Understanding and Advancing the Self

Other books by Ashok Tyagi*

- **All About Hinduism**
  From Vedas to Devas and Past to Present

- **All About Spirituality**
  Practical Ways for Self Realisation

- **All About Meditation**
  Art and Science of Fulfillment ans Euphpria

*Kindle editions also available

Understanding and Advancing the Self

Ashok Tyagi

SHIPRA

₹ 350
US$ 10.40
ISBN: 978-93-91978-22-8

First Published in India in 2023

Understanding and Advancing the Self

Published by:
SHIPRA PUBLICATIONS
LG 18-19, Pankaj Central Market
I.P. Ext., Patparganj, Delhi 110092, India
Tel.: +91 11 2223 5152/6152; 96500 28065
E-mail: info@shiprapublication.com
www.shiprapublication.com

Contents

Introduction

"If you begin to understand what you are without trying to change it, then what you are undergoes a transformation." —J. Krishnamurti

Every human being is a unique combination of instincts, hopes, aspirations, memories, experiences, feelings, thoughts, insecurities, fears, frustrations, values, dogmas, beliefs, attitudes, emotions, sense of morality, sense of ethics, empathy and systems encompassing all of above. To make matter worse, this entity remains a work in process, changing all the time and getting multiplied into roles such as a student, a friend, a player, a worker, a parent or member to a group. We also come in contacts with other individuals having varying degree of similarities or differences from ours on each counts mentioned above. This constant crisscrossing impresses and get impressed upon our own self. Interestingly, all characteristics, features, or values, beliefs, opinions used in defining us are not even chosen by us. Those features may or may not be aligned with our intrinsic self.

A majority live life without complete and accurate understanding about their inner essence or their intrinsic core. Understanding of a normal person about self is based on his/her perceptions formed through layers and layers of experiences, borrowed knowledge and impressions accumulated over life. Since those perceptions get formed on multiple-coloured shades of subjectivity, real self remains buried down tons of misunderstandings. Real self happens to be subtle, unlimited, and eternal. Gaining full access to that real self is, however, difficult because it is shy, has a very feeble voice, its suggestions are reticent, and its language is very crisp.

Without doubt, the subject, Understanding the Self, is complex and intricate as it involves poking around in a fog, and that too with a long stick because self is best observed from a distance. Let us begin by saying that self is much more than physical body, mind, intellect and some other features and traits that make all above elements work together in harmony. Self is not something static as it keeps evolving with every passing moment. One may also not bracket self clearly in black or white as it has many shades of grey in between. Self is also circumstantial and multidimensional which is largely influenced by time and mental state one holds at the time of his commentary about it.

In current context, understanding self is intended to help reader improve productivity, make relations stronger with others around, gain better physical health, and become better in occupation or profession one is engaged in. Besides practical and tangible benefits, its contribution towards advancement of 'psychological or spiritual quotient', may be taken as icing on the cake. To that extent, the context of this all-pervading ancient question of "Who am I", for our endeavor in hand, has much modern nuance focused on the direct and immediate, visible and verifiable, here and now. In brief, understanding self assures practical and tangible benefits related to individual as well as social well-being in general and as a significant effective tool for an all-important 'self-improvement project' in particular.

Significance of gaining access to Self, in this background, using all available tools and techniques possible, gains critical importance. Connecting with your Self is something of a paradox because while you are physically always connected, establishing unity with it remains a lifelong struggle. Understanding this very self, however, got transformational possibilities of immense dimensions. As soon as that happens, you are assured of incredibly flashes of intuition, imaginations and inspiration, the virtues that make you unique. No wonder, comprehension and proper development of self is said to be one of the greatest journeys one ever undertakes.

This journey calls for developing right understanding of your entire complex entity, including all parts and subparts irrespective of those being good or bad, peaceful or violent, cruel or wicked. Exploring self involves taking on all these parts irrespective of shame or pains involved. Self needs to be approached with an explorative keenness to observe entire spectrum of existence just like a video camera records all happening without differentiating between event being happy or sad. Access to self doesn't come as a gift, blessing or in inheritance. This access can, however, be gained by anyone showing curiosity, devotion and commitment to do so.

This book highlights factors contributing the formation of Self by explaining critical roles of family, teachers and other critical socio-cultural-religious factors. The book highlights associated concepts of self to help decode the bigger picture. In the process, many doubts and preconceived notions, capable of creating serious roadblocks, are also properly dealt with. This book unfolds ways and means to establish complete understanding of all critical issues involved in the journey while living normal life, juggling pressures of career, family and society at large. Off course, the process presupposes you being awfully adaptive, masterful un-learner and avid learner. The mind interested in diving deep within must have aversion in taking things on face value. You better be open and skeptical at the same time.

As a first stage objective, this book spells out ways to sharpen vision for focusing on Self, know its reality, accept that reality as it exists, and finally making peace with that reality. During this process, people come across areas that they may not be happy about, where they discern changes required. The book also lays out required 'dos' and 'don'ts' to be learnt and mastered to see the bright light at the end of that long tunnel. Finally, the reader is exposed as to how to make amend to all undesirable elements, one by one, so that the process of knowing self fructify and deliver practical benefits.

Finally, this book can be used in multiple ways. It provides very detailed course material covering all aspects of concepts rolled out. The book helps its readers to know themselves through unblemished and genuinely clean lenses, thereby helping them in living a blissful human life in harmony with everything and everyone around. The book can also be used as a compass to check direction of the progress made. It can also be considered a troubleshooting guide if and when the reader faces roadblocks in making desired progress or seeking course correction midway. Finally, the book seeks to help the reader graduate to the level of practical self-realization.

Self exploration happens to be a perfectly neutral subject and usual known differentiations of gender, age, religion, language, education etc. do not play any role here. As such, the mention of the reader as 'he' throughout this book is just for the sake of brevity and it always include users of all genders without any differentiation.

It will be pleasure to receive your views, feedback and suggestions, if any, at indotyagi@gmail.com

Part I

1

Evolution of Self

Self and its Significance

> *"You are iron plated gold, running here and there to save yourself from rust. Stop identifying with the thin layer of iron; you are the gold underneath."*

The concept of understanding self in the form of the popular question "Who am I" initially originated in a philosophical or spiritual context. Normal people could simply brush aside this question and carry on living daily mundane life. However, in modern times, and in current context, we initially plan to understand and use the answer to this question for gaining practical and tangible benefits related to individual as well as social well-being in general and as a significant effective tool for an all-important 'self-improvement project' in particular.

In that background, understanding self will be appreciated so long as it helps us improving our productivity, make our relations stronger with others around, helps us gaining better physical health, and enhances our knowledge for discussing among friends. These are all too familiar issues that impact our life on daily basis, here and now. After enjoying practical and tangible benefits, its contribution towards advancement of 'psychological or spiritual quotient', will be taken as an add on.

Connecting with Self being a Difficult Choice

The process of exploring Self works as the most effective reminder that enhances our ability to receive signals that life is timeless. It makes us realize that we are part of eternal consciousness and occupy this body/mind entity only temporarily. But, speaking generally, the life vortex proves too tempting and seductive stonewalling reminders coming from within. The feeble sound of conscience gets more often interrupted from reaching to our ears. On the other hand, conscious awareness is inherently still, shy and silent. Without perfect internal as well as external silence, you cannot even experience it or feel it in any way. Many people live full physical life without ever listening to this unique silence, and it has been so all over our recorded history.

The exercise of 'Understanding Self' asks us to replace our 'current perception' with 'correct comprehension'. It asks us to behave responsibly and see through the web of desires and attractions controlling our behaviors and thinking patterns. Understanding real self helps in taking responsibility of achieving our full potential (high or low, desirable or worth criticism) rather than blame our failures or limitations on extraneous factors like genes, brain's biochemistry, constellation at birth, upbringing, immediate environment or even external pressures.

Understanding Self brings a new option of re-engineering oneself and not to allow these issues limit one's potential. Agreed that thinking, feelings, actions occupying us are just a matter of habit flowing through our existence like free-flowing powerful rivers. But the choice of flowing with the current, and allowing streams take us wherever, or decide about own destination, even when it involves swimming against the current, lies purely with us. This choice separates adults from teenagers or special from ordinary and makes us qualify to become first among equals. Agreed that going against the currents demand a great deal of preparedness but that is how real winners are tested.

Process of Understanding Self in Brief

Knowing about self is a long-drawn process and involves a lot of commitment, dedication and will power. This process throws up great deal of impurity and dirt accumulated in untrained minds. Making those impurities settle down naturally demand a great deal of cleansing commensurate with the dirt accumulated. Such an effort demands working on several aspects before expecting significant changes begin to accrue. It calls for removing layers and layers of unwanted overgrowth of ignorance or wrong knowledge and replacing them with correct knowledge and right perceptions. This process also demands work on many allied concepts like improving compassion, empathy, morality and ethics.

The only equipment and entire laboratory required for exploring self is nothing but our own mind. Real success of this exercise requires work on two streams simultaneously. On one hand, one must reprocess stored experiences and memories in order to remove all shades of biases or mistaken impressions. On the other hand, one must install a strong security system for proper gatekeeping to allow only desired thoughts gaining entry in the mind. Self-exploration is also known to impact a great deal of emotional, philosophical, psychological and spiritual churning, with their respective challenges. The person interested to travel this path, therefore, must get prepared to deal with many unknowns on the way. One is also advised to start work on this project without too many preconceived perceptions because all perceptions eventually grow to become definite roadblocks hampering right progress.

You begin this journey by

- first practicing to achieve stillness of mind even when silence scares.
- making peace with your imperfections staring back at you.
- learning to be completely truthful to yourself and develop your impartial gaze on your own self for every facet of your life (including the good, bad and the ugly), without any evaluation or explanation.
- developing courage for looking at what you are and not what you thought you were, or as told by others, or desired to be.
- developing access to your hidden triggers for motivation, love, hate and passions, and that too, in dispassionate manner.

You discover yourself in the relationships, in the process, you will also look at all your relationships. This is required to know yourself through others and the vice versa. After all, you cannot know others well until you know yourself as well. There are a number of aspects of life that cannot be seen except with the help of other people. You do require others to work as your mirrors to feed you with their insights and perspectives. Other people alone tell us about our hard-to-see parts.

Finally, you will have to face and fight all your fears, doubts, dilemmas, disillusionments and frustrations. It is indeed a rewarding journey as people travelling before report enjoying mesmerizing scenery on the sides. Incidentally, the need to know about own self is much more relevant today than any other time in the past. More people depend on self-ignitions today than ever. So called social, political and economic progress takes more people away from their roots embedded in family and friends than before. As a result, self-knowledge is much more important today to guide actions, hierarchy and codes. Deeper understanding of self certainly proves beneficial in exploiting newfound freedom and independence.

Caution against Over-expectations from Understanding Self

Expecting understanding of self to work as a solution to all problems of normal life is wrong *ab initio*. No doubt deeper knowledge brings transformational changes in life but continuation of all its benefits is inversely correlated with continuation of negative activities like stress, anger, envy, lust, bond with materialism and attachments. Let us remember that everything, small and big, happening in our normal life has impact on progress we make in our exploration of Self. Even if we get to see glimpse of Self, returning back to living life like before is going to erode all the gains sooner than later.

'Self' not being Body or Mind

Physical body of a person is the surest and most obvious sign of his existence. That is the precise reason of every person getting identified with his body more than anything else. Body can be touched and felt in many interesting ways. It gets associated with the name and works as an address when other people wish to reach us. Limbs of the body and its sensory system make one aware about the entire universe. It is functional and movable and sustains entire life in general. No wonder, people remain attached with it, attend to its requirements and invest time, attention and energy on its looks, forms and decoration. Finally, it consists of highly complex systems and functions like the best of machines around. But it certainly falls short of defining the power behind it, the Self.

Human body is indeed a uniquely temporary composition. Every cell of human body gets replaced over a maximum of twelve years period. If we look at it on elemental level, ninety-nine per cent of the body mass consists of oxygen, carbon, hydrogen, calcium and phosphorus. On atomic level, entire body and its processes can be broken down to atoms, which are made up of interacting subatomic particles, and can be called as 'matter' for general discussions. Interestingly, all elements of 'matter' are always temporary and are known to change its combinations all the time. Similarly, body's functional systems like Digestive and Excretory, Cardiovascular and Respiratory, Nervous and Immune, Skeletal and Muscular, or systems relating to Reproduction, are by and large independent in their respective working and sustain life without much intervention. These very processes also generate multiple sensations like pain, hunger, thirst, injury, tiredness, fear, and pleasures, etc. All these systems have been serving humanity over long period, operate on fairly uniform basis and do not differ much from person to person. The reply to the question of their correlation with our uniqueness is firmly negative as most human share them collectively.

Yes, our body is a machine that allows us experiencing this world in physical form similar to a vehicle used for undertaking a particular journey. To ensure a safe ride, comfortable sitting and enjoying passing scenery, one takes care of the vehicle all through the journey and keep attending to its maintenance and fuel demands but, no matter what, after the end of the journey, that very vehicle gets parked and left alone in some corner. Vehicle's size, make, shine, appearance, color and all other features never remain relevant after arrival on the destination. For sure, nobody will factor in the features on vehicle used to arrive with defining the purpose of the journey. So human body is an amazingly complex entity, serves us all through our life span, but is not what we are. We call the body as 'our body' but not 'we the body'.

Self not being the Mind Either

Some people consider mind as main component of existence and explain that a person is a mind having a body at its service. Body and mind are surely connected but theirs is rather an awkward relationship. Modern day neuroscience has proven beyond doubts that all systems and subsystems working inside human mind are purely physical elements, conceptually and casually embedded in the natural world. Human mind receives very large number internal signals besides sense organs constantly relaying very large sensations providing mind the linkage with external world. Mind certainly remains super occupied in processing those sensations aided by already stored experiences, memories and impressions. It's imagination, thinking, intuition and strategic planning attributes also help it to factor projections for time to come.

Many people believe mind to be a unique collection of memories, experiences, feelings, opinions or beliefs. They say that we are what we think and thereby hold mind in supreme position. But to quote modern neuroscience again, thoughts and emotions are purely work of hormones like testosterone. Mind does create all thoughts through its inextricable links with the body and the surrounding environment. Thoughts and feelings are also momentary in nature and are influenced by other things like personal attitudes, aptitudes, imaginations, and impressions of both self and people one interacts with. Beliefs and opinions get formed randomly, are generally not set in concrete and can be seen changing all the time.

Memories, similarly, are foggy. One's recollection of same incidence of the past is invariably colored by his mood at the time of recall. Opinions also fall in ever changing basket as you can see people changing opinions with every change of hat they wear. Opinions are nothing but ways in which people attempt to link themselves to a given situation, issue, time and circumstance. Invariably, change in any of those underlying condition brings change in opinions as well. Similarly, thoughts generated by mind also result from interplay of emotions, intellect, memory and ego, which are always non-permanent in character, and fail to define an individual as a unique identity. Opinions and beliefs, in any case, describe only specific elements about a person, nothing beyond.

Mind's working is best compared with giant size computer server that operates in line with its software(s) installed (and updated from time to time) and data base created during its years in use. Even when human mind is established as more complex than other machines, its reality doesn't change a bit. Because all machines, at the end of the day, are just machines. They can be built, operated, maintained, used, refurbished, reproduced or scrapped any time by their makers or owners. Under any situation, a machine can never be identified with a unique identity that any human being happens to be.

Interestingly, human mind does not even operate under the control of its owners. It seldom behaves the way its master commands it. If the mind was to operate under direction of its owners, it should obey all commands at all times and should surrender to the will of its owner without resistance. But mind is rebellion, disobeys all the time and hates to operate under rules and regulations. Just try asking it to focus its attention on a subject of your choice and you are destined to disappointments seeing it fleeting fast and behaving in disorderly manner. Attempts to bring it under control expose its monkey nature time and again. It loves jumping from one thought to another and remains engaged working on its own agenda. It embarrasses you ever so regularly whenever you ask it to avoid entertaining thoughts and feelings you wish to avoid. It keeps proving the saying 'mind has a mind of its own' true on most occasions.

Looking closely, one realizes human mind being similar to a vast ocean. Human mind has undercurrents operating at all times. In that gigantic body of water, the existence of a tiny entity "I" is similar to a tiny little boat struggling to continue floating somehow. So, the mind can be anything but that very helpless 'I' we are trying to establish link with reference to Self. As it is, mind is a process and not a state; mind is a verb and not a noun; mind is a journey and not a destination; mind can be trained and enlightened, albeit, with concentration, patience and tons of efforts. If rest of the body is gross physical body, mind is just a subtle material body. It also comes with 'use before' date as it does become weak slowly but eventually.

Interestingly, at times we tend to look at things going on in our mind from purely a third-party perspective. On such occasions we also listen to a feeble voice suggesting us to do the right thing, the voice of our conscience. So, if we can see ourselves from a distance or if we can have a pure independent voice well within our own self, and we are able to process such observation and pure counsel within our own mind, surely, we cannot be that very mind. The 'observer' and the one 'observed' ought to be different entities. Surely, the 'self' we are searching is different from our mind and cannot be the constant and abiding entity that we know we are.

Besides body and mind, even one's relationships with other people around also do not define a person in any significant way. Other people interacting with us look at us as a 'name card' where they relate with us with reference to our distinct name, job title, relationship status or membership of a particular group, which may be social, religious, political or sports. Even this vast bouquet is nothing but collection of several flowers representing particular aspects and, at best, make us a collection of multiple identities. While we may agree that these identities may contribute in bits and pieces to define who we are, these can never represent the whole of us. Any attempt to link 'self' with some or all of these identities always falls short and remains incomplete.

What We really are

Besides body, mind and changing identities discussed above, there certainly exists another aspect that feels, judges, reflects and anticipates. This aspect may not be visible but without this both body and mind entity get reduced to being just a big mix of matter. One may also associate this active aspect with 'the voice in our head'. This is the aspect that is known by multiple names such as soul, consciousness, conscience, life breath, or 'atman'. Some modern thinkers also call it by the name of 'conscious awareness'. They define 'self' simply as a form that is aware.

Everything else is explained as simply projections of life situations. This force is the real principle of life, got distinct entity, never changes, and remains with us all through our life including when we sleep, dream or even when we are actually unaware. This 'awareness' is completely different than all mental processes involved in thoughts, actions, memories or feelings. This very element is immortal and is beyond time or space. This also is the spiritual part of human. That is how we are called spiritual being having human experience.

Probing How much We Know about Ourselves

A very learned person said that "to know oneself by oneself is to dream a dream within a dream and simultaneously remember all the details of that dream without being part of the dream". This statement reflects reality and cannot be brushed aside. Proven by psychological research, the fact remains that most people do not have the privilege to know their own reality. Ignorant knowledge about self may appear as reality because it gets built overtime. Our internal senses link us to the world and the awareness so created stand between us and our real identity. Unfortunately, majority of people are just ok for living life even with their foggy existence. "Reality bites" and most people do not even make an attempt to uncover real identity.

Under this background, the readers may be excited to check their own standing about their individual experience of own self. Results obtained from such realization will pave way for the seriousness with which their endeavor of understanding self is taken up. To be fair, you should not be forced to make all efforts to understand yourself better if you already have fair amount of comprehension about yourself. On the other hand, if a person fails to score well, he is expected to see the dichotomy and commit himself hard to pursue the journey lying ahead. So, let us get ready for this interesting test to figure out how intimately you are aware about none other than your own self.

For this test, however, you are going to play dual role of an examiner and examinee. Certainly, it is no mean feat and does ask for some exclusive preparations. In order to do justice to your dual role, please imagine coming out of your physical body for a while. Just imagine as if you have placed your mental image at an altar/

table, a little distance in front of your body. Having seated comfortably, please look intuitively at your erstwhile entity, take up each of the following questions, one at a time, and think carefully, remaining true to your intellect. Please do not get surprised by the randomness of the questions as it is purposefully designed so. Also, do not worry, if you come across a little bit of repetition or overlapping, and just limit your evaluation to that specific question alone, as if that is the only question at that point of time.

Some of these questions also have additional complimentary parts. You are supposed to count the whole as one question and factor all the parts while arriving at your evaluations. Since there are several questions and you may not be able to do it in single sitting, please repeat the ritual explained above, every time you come back to your test time. In the likelihood of a question not being applicable to you, please move over to the next without scoring. In final analysis, such questions may also be deducted from total number of questions. Use the scale of 'zero to ten' where a complete denial equals to zero, partial denial between one to five and partial agreement ranging between six to nine and explicit agreement scores a perfect ten. Basically, scoring follows your degree of agreement from low to high.

However, if you are a person of qualitative mind, you may attempt to answer the questions based on your qualitative assessment. In that case, you can assign your reply as A, B, C or D where 'A' stands for 'Not True', 'B' stands for 'Somewhat Untrue' and 'C' stands for 'Somewhat True' and finally 'D' standing for 'Very True' conclusions.

All questions mentioned below have been framed to help you detect presence of grey areas that you may be living with in normal day to day life. The questions cover critical issues impacting life in variety of areas like self-awareness, logical thinking, application of reasoning, normal attitude towards life, your foundations of morality and ethics, your empathy quotient, awareness for your likes/dislikes, your sources of inspiration, emotional balance, triggers for excitation, your ambitions and aspirations, your sense of self-reliance, contribution in team workings, dependence on others, your self-conceptualization, degree displayed for flexibility and adaptability, and so on.

Let us begin to check how intimately you know yourself.

Understanding the Self — A Questionnaire

Sl. No.	*Question asked about your own self*	*Score*
1.	You do have a set criterion for selecting friends and you apply those filters without exception. You also periodically re-evaluate that eligibility for people to let them continue within your circle of closeness or push them out of your circle of closeness.	
2.	You can convincingly come up with precise five words that describe your own perceived understanding of self. This is the same list that was existing even five or ten years ago.	

3. You are logically very sure about how much you know about yourself. You never found your self- understanding lacking in any way as you know as much as you would ever like to know.
4. You never discriminate people based on their gender, class, caste, height, body type, skin color, race, region, language spoken, culture or religion. You never have any pre-existing image of people and deal with a new person in absolute impartial manner.
5. You do not succumb under peer pressure and never go along with friends in doing things you would not do yourself.
6. You can convincingly list out top five unique strength that distinguishes you from other persons of your age, education, family background and profession.
7. You are clearly aware and can list out top five weaknesses that have held you back from making greater success in life.
8. If you ever get confined in an unorganized place, no matter for how long, but you will never feel comfortable in that kind of place. You will do your best to organize the place before starting to work.
9. You are absolutely sure of your favorite color in clothes, flowers and paintings. You also have your reasoning as why you like what you like. You are also certain the combination of colors that you like and why.
10. You never take decisions in jiffy. Irrespective of situation, you always collect all information, check all facts and slowly arrive at a well thought out decision. Your decision-making approach can't be termed as risk taking. Rather it can clearly be called cautious and calculated.
11. You are aware of your unique skill sets. You do qualify being in top 20% category for those special skills within your limited area of influence. (If you are a cricketer - you play for your state, if you are a Lawyer - you win 80% of your cases, if you are a doctor - you get counted as top ten specialist of your district, if you are a CA - your firm falls in top 20% firms of your city, and so on)
12. You are a lone wolf and perform higher when you work alone but you never lose interest when forced to work in a group. When in group, you contribute to improve performance of your colleagues as well.
13. While sitting on dining table with friends, you often pass dishes to others and rarely ask others to do that for you. You always hesitate in disturbing others for your work.
14. You are able to perform at your peak productivity even in a crowded environment as you can adjust your internal systems and avoid adverse impacts of external environment. A peaceful surrounding is hardly essential for you.
15. Faced with stiff competition, you do not feel the pang of fears but only excitement to excel. You always focus on putting your best irrespective of what others are doing in that situation.
16. You are fully aware about how you chose your role models and other influencers. Your heroes and influencers remain constant across

timelines. Known divisions like geographical boundaries, political lineage or religious moorings do not play any part in your selection.

17. You are sure of your process for arriving at your top choices for movies, books, sport person, music pieces, and other such pass time activities. You do that with solid reasons. The process you apply is fair, consistent, logical and neutral.
18. Career/occupation is important to you and you wish to grow to its pinnacle but you will never compromise or ignore priorities for comforts of family members for betterment of career.
19. Whenever told to follow given instructions, you are at ease and embrace them judiciously without any feeling of rebellion. You are a perfect conformist when it comes to following rules and regulations.
20. On a day of heavy workload, you prefer waking up early and starting work early instead of waking at normal time and extending your schedule towards the end of your day.
21. You do possess specific sets of values and with reason. You are often guided by your own values and goals and not the values of people falling in your close circle.
22. You speak out loud every time you come across bias and intolerance and stand up against the perpetrators rather than turning a blind eye or ignoring the same.
23. Because time is more important to you, wherever applicable, you prefer to spend higher money to save time and not vice versa.
24. You do not resort to speaking lie under any situation, not even during negotiations of financial nature or performance results of self or family.
25. You are ardent advocate of practicing patience. And you can give any number of examples where you indeed preferred patience over impatience.
26. Given a demand coming from unknown people, you always feel happy to extend help with money/time or your expertise/experience. Under any situation, you never flatly refuse extending help in one or the other form.
27. Out of alternate options of 'yes' and 'no', you end up using 'no' more often as you do not want others to remain in any doubt. You never make false promise of giving help to others when you do not intend to really help.
28. You have definite names of people who charge your energy level to do bigger and better. Similarly, you clearly recognize people capable of inspiring you or charging you positively as well as people making you exhausted or violent.
29. Under the unfortunate situation of a fire at your house, you are absolutely sure of the top three things you would like to salvage.
30. When you come across your mistakes or shortcomings, you always feel responsible for them and seek forgiveness from impacted people irrespective they being your juniors or subordinates.

31. You are absolutely certain about your top five personal milestones which may be termed as your moments of climbing your own personal Mount Everest.
32. You can clearly list out all possible situations, jobs or people that you wish to avoid.
33. You are perfectly aware of the things that you do not wish to lose. Also, you have similar clarity about things that you never going to regret losing.
34. You are fully apprehensive of wasting your spare time. No, you do not spend more than allotted time to checking messages, videos or pictures posted by unknown people on social media.
35. You set time limits and adhere to set durations for your access to your social media plate forms on day-to-day basis.
36. Emotions and moods do impact your general behavior. You can clearly list out five emotions having strong impact on the way you generally behave.
37. You do not hesitate in voicing your opinions even when they may be different than people you admire or love. And you hold no feeling when those dear ones do not agree with your opinion.
38. You can always list out unwanted episodes with family members, relatives, friends, co-workers, neighbors or acquaintances for which you often feel regrets.
39. Your perspective towards external world in normal and your view on future in particular falls under healthy category as against being branded as neutral or gloomy.
40. You clearly can recall five instances in last thirty days when you made specific efforts to make things better and pleasant for your significant other. You are always aware about your individual responsibilities, specially, towards immediate family members.
41. You wish your son/daughter to be like the son/daughter you are to your parents and you wish your spouse to be in no way different than the kind of spouse you are to him/her. You believe more in giving than taking when it comes to personal relations.
42. You do not suffer from repetitive thought patterns as you are good at pushing useless things out of your mind as and when you chose to do so. You normally entertain only thoughts that you wish and not random thoughts picked up by mind.
43. You do not get stressed out from thinking about things out of your control where you have no individual role to contribute towards the outcome of events to come.
44. You are good at setting goals voluntarily and often keep working until set goals get achieved.
45. You maintain clear list of five things/issues/subjects that you find yourself passionate about.

46. You are very happy about your work as it is able to attract your full attention and it happens to be something that really fulfills you completely. To you work actually feels like hobby.
47. You prefer to handle difficult and strong people in a straightforward and direct manner rather than resorting to diplomacy or tact.
48. You do maintain very clearly defined targets towards physical health parameters, mental health, career progress, family's welfare, personal growth, financial stability and materialistic possessions in general.
49. You can clearly note down couple of things that you hate to do at home during your free time and things that you hate to do while at work.
50. You are very passionate about getting what you set your eye on and are willing to compromise means for ends as you feel committed to go to any length to get what you want.

At this stage, we were looking about your own perceptions about your own self. Interestingly, at this stage we have not even brought in the gap that inevitably exists between your perceptions of your reality and the real reality. As a result, there is no point in commenting about the total scores earned. As such, the scoring need not be taken very seriously. It was just a ploy to force you take a serious view about your understanding so that serious analysis can be carried out, if and when required. Basic objective is to let you prick deep, force to think through and revisit your own impressions.

"Finding yourself is not really how it works. You aren't a ten-dollar bill in last winter's coat pocket. You are also not lost. Your true self is right there, buried under cultural conditioning, other people's opinions, and inaccurate conclusions you drew as a kid that became your beliefs about who you are. "Finding yourself" is actually returning to yourself. An unlearning, an excavation, a remembering who you were before the world got its hands on you."

— Emily McDowell

Factors Affecting Evolution of Self: Family, School and Society

Very concept of Self is a complex web of the person's behaviors, associations, genetics, roles, responsibilities, and attitudes. Contrary to common belief, no one is born with all these attributes. Only a select few of these are inherited genetically. These attributes are largely acquired during growing process through interactions with various influencers in one's life. Later, even during adulthood, this process never stops altogether. Experiences gained while working for occupations, hobbies, affiliations, and working in other socio-economic-religious-spiritual spheres, also keep contributing bit-by-bit or keep cementing earlier formed attributes. That is why it is always called as work in process. These get formed similar to the strokes applied by a painter on his canvass to convert it into a unique painting. Be it childhood, adolescence or adulthood, irrespective of age brackets, people keep borrowing impressions which get invested towards developing one's uniqueness and continue reflecting in his Self of the moment.

Besides the immediate family, most critical of all these factors are society we operate in, the cultural landscape we belong to, as also the pressures exerted by peers and colleagues. Initially, parents and immediate family provide foundation for evolution of values and attitudes. Parents are also responsible for transferring cultural influence on the child. Later that process gets reinforced at school with teachers and fellow students. Still later, when one starts mingling with external environment, many of the earlier formed values get revisited or reconstructed under influence of society and environment in general. Interactions or simply knowing about views of role models coming from across spectrum, together with the understanding of the working of this world, offer yet another phase of reshaping or re-clarification of our abilities, preferences, attitudes, values and individual beliefs. In that sense, the entire concept of self is quite an open-ended constructive process which keep getting revised and re-descripting all over our childhood to matured adulthood.

While there are many individual factors for evolution of self, it will be interesting to look at each of the major influencer category is some details. The twin objective here are to sharpen own understanding of the influencing factors and simultaneously comprehending what we should do when we play role as an influencer for others going through their shaping under our wings. Let us follow the organic route of aging from the childhood to becoming a responsible adult.

1. Role of Parents and Family

The evolution of self gets initiated from early stages of childhood. A child learns maximum from his parents, grandparents, siblings and other immediate family members living around him. Interactions with family help a child make sense of things around, working of punishment and rewards mechanism, inference of right and wrong actions as well as his own identity. Interactions with parents and family also provide confidence to the child about his basic competencies enabling him to deal with normal challenges of life. Their encouragement and appreciation sow initial seeds of self-confidence and self-esteem.

Parents also shape initial meaning of self-worth of a child. They provide him reasons to feel worthy of happiness. Sense of self-esteem is not offered by parents on a plate, but their style of raising the child can certainly remove obstacles coming in child's way of building positive self-esteem. Parents and immediate family work as roots for their children ensuring stability and providing nutrition for physical, mental, social and psychological growth. Above all, family also offer children wings to fly. All subsequent structures of self-confidence and self-worth get built on the foundation provided by immediate family.

Family settings provide crucial environment where child's entire value system takes shape. Ways of the family treating its young at home, shape his expectations from rest of the world. Later he also starts dealing with others using same values. The affection, attention and care evolved within a positive family atmosphere prepares the child to offer love, respect and compassion to the external world in general. Usual hugging and kissing are proper declaration of parents love for their loved ones. Until a child starts understanding language words in proper perspective, physical intimacy conveys him sense of love, support, care and nurturing. Touching is known to send sensory stimulations resulting in faster mental development of a child. On the other hand, absence of affection and clarity sow seeds of self-doubts and self-distrust. How can a child fraught with such negative traits ever be successful in his later life?

When parents and other family members treat a child with courtesy, respect and benevolence, the child automatically learns to imbibe those very values in his own actions and responses. Actual behavior of the family with a child is his first center of learning. It is wrong to believe that as an infant the child is immune to things like appreciation, affection or respect. An infant recognizes the touch and smell of his mother within first couple of weeks on this earth. Thereafter his understanding for all feelings keeps evolving slowly but surely. A child needs care as well as respect and he understand these feelings fair and square. How can one ignore the frustrations of a toddler conveyed through crying when his requirements are not taken seriously or urgently?

At times, a parent shows lack of patience while a child struggles to convey his point in his incoherent style and gets cuts off. What do you think will happen to his confidence and esteem? Cutting off by a parent or attempt to divert child's attention to some other issue, under above situation, get noticed by the child in no uncertain terms. That child is bound to feel insufficient, unloved and insignificant. But we see ignorant parents resorting to such things all around. Family is advised to look in the eyes of the child while he speaks and should never cut him off midway. Even a child has developed sense for both impatience and lack of interest displayed by an elder. If a child is not allowed to have a voice in his own affairs, we cannot expect him to feel entitled to his own views when he grows up as an adult.

As parents, we can make efforts to inspire our children before expecting or demanding results from them. Love, acceptance and respect offered to a child goes in generating powerful sense of self and vice versa. We should encourage our child to undergo a bit of struggle in his actions. That struggle is key for developing his sense of achievement. A child protected against normal struggles is also not exposed to the virtue of winning which is so important for success in adult life. Struggle feeds the seeds for problem solving zeal in later life and thereby fuels success.

Parents and other family members also play a key role in supporting curiosity in the young ones. All innocent questions raised by kids need be replied seriously and certainly in a non-dismissive manner. No question from a child be taken as silly or trivial if you wish to fuel his curiosity. Let us remember that this world and its ways are still new for a child. His asking questions must be a welcome celebration as it suggests that he is thinking and is showing interest in primary learning.

And it is not that a parent is not allowed to express disappointment or anger. But let it be done with love and respect kept intact. Worst signal sent to a child is withdrawal or physical abuse. Please make efforts for teaching to them without letting them develop sense of rejection or insufficiency. It is proven that normal things that work for adults (like arguing, lecturing, shaming or insulting) completely fail in case of children. Even psychologizing or bargaining doesn't cut ice with kids. Do not forget that only a child treated with respect is expected to grow self-respect and that criticism is possible with respect kept intact.

Some parents are seen appreciating smallest achievement of their children as if some great achievement is made. This is obviously very detrimental to his sense of achievement. Out of proportion appreciation runs the risk of spoiling child's sense of accomplishment and certainly adds to his hesitation. Such uncertain sense achievement is going to kill his ambition for achieving big. Parents need to be aware of such danger with absolute clarity. Sense of proportion remains ever so important. Opting for tall appreciation for normal ordinary things, you are only fueling their sense of confusion. Finally, the biggest favor we can do as parents is to help our child grow his sense of self by asking questions that stimulate his thinking. It is done by abstaining to ask questions which can be replied in simple yes or no. Always rephrase your questions to let your child go in thinking mode. Habit of thinking is the best gift that parents can bestow on their children.

Lastly, developing self is more about living than learning. Let your child's inner state fill with clarity, love and self-respect and guide them as their own shadow all through their journey into adolescence. The inner light once illuminated is completely capable of supporting your child as an unseen guide for all times to come.

2. Role of Teachers and Schools

Schools truly represents second best opportunity to children for developing virtues contributing towards forming and sustaining of self. School teachers can wipe out scars of a student who, for some reasons, got deprived of love and secure environment at home. Good school environment always proves helpful for children to acquire a better self and develop a positive vision of future life. Teachers have power to work as an antidote to do away dents made by a family that failed to inject confidence in the competence and goodness of their child.

School education must provide a foundation to the students in the basics needed to function effectively in the modern world. Alas, many schools are still stuck with outdated curriculum and are not well equipped in ensuring building strong foundation. The entire syllabus is seen focusing on better academic scores and excelling of some external factors. Schooling, particularly in countries like India, remain focused on how to work rather than how to think. There are neither courses nor teachers focusing on developing critical thinking among their wards. How long can we avoid teaching 'how to think'? Thinking is expected to boost self-esteem and self-confidence and help the child face the challenges of life head on.

Prevailing academic system the world over seems to be failing in appreciating that advancing self is also an acquirable skill and presumably step by step instructions available to a beginner may help him grow his Self in a systematic manner. Unlike some new popular skill that gets picked up under parental pressure or for making lucrative career choices, advancing self needs personal attention of teachers on one-on-one basis. Agreed that scope and significance of teachers vary from skill to skill but only personalized attention from teachers can provide step-by-step directions to young students while they unfold deeper potentialities of their minds. And unlike performing arts like acting, singing, music or even cooking, where the role of a teacher is just limited to introduce his wards to basics or provide just the technical knowledge about the subject, advancing self requires a very active role of a teacher. Promoting self is entirely a different area where instructions and guidance have smaller capacitance.

The real requirement for advancing self is to grow unique muscles for working in the areas of esteem, confidence, attitude, aptitudes and general world view. Most of these attributes revolve around internal affairs of a ward. So, growing these muscles require cultivation of a unique innate ability where outside guidance is of not much use. But this is not to say that teachers have no role at all. That will be utter injustice. An experienced teacher giving individual attention on a ward may very well observe his hidden personal traits and can effectively provide useful inputs. But such personal attention gets largely overlooked in a classroom setting. Unfortunately, most issues impacting growth of self are very subtle in nature and get stimulated through churning going inside a young mind. And unlike any time in history, application of mental faculties, honed on pure thinking, is proving most important today at jobs and occupations as well. Hence, enabling better thinking, creativity and innovativeness will help advancing self as well as careers of children when they move into their adulthoods.

Besides facilitating organized thinking, another area where schools and teachers can play equally bigger role is to expose children to whole gamut of deeper understanding of feelings. A good teacher will always teach his students respect for rational feelings and how to withstand even situations where feelings are unfavorable to their liking. Children must be taught ill effects of allowing feelings and emotions ruling responses. If normal life going to be filled with turbulences of feelings and emotions, schools must gear up to make children capable for going over them with success. For example, it is true that there was no need to teach ill effects of stress and tensions thirty years back, but today's children must be made well equipped to face these new menaces fair and square. Similar arguments apply to make students capable for dealing with evils of social media and computer-based gaming which has gained popularity in recent times. Technology is bringing new issues by the day and schools have to live up for all such emerging issues.

Fortunately, many states and communities are recognizing the importance of best possible attention required for their young minds. They can be seen hiring the best of their people to work as primary school teachers precisely because most of the critical learning, thinking included, is imparted to children while they are still in primary standards. A qualified and vigilant primary teacher can do wonders in introducing a child with his better self at his formative stage itself. Such teachers believe that they are there to build future of their societies and take pride in their job much different than any normal occupation.

There is a particular expectation from teachers who come across children from variety of backgrounds and life experiences. It is especially important for you to understand cultural influence of identity of your wards and combine that knowledge with individual differences of your students. As a teacher you must provide your students and their families with culturally and developmentally sensitive care and help them become successful in their later years. You can do wonders for proper assimilation of children coming from different backgrounds by main streaming them with care and without inflicting deep scratches.

In the ancient past, students in India used to attend Gurukuls. Gurukuls are known for providing focus on imparting all round knowledge including principles, ethics, and morality of a particular tradition they belonged. Gurukuls never remained limited to offer only formal education to their wards. Only some Gurukuls were admitting wards from royal families where specific emphasis was provided mainly on warcraft and statecraft besides shaping entire world view of the wards. But these were rather exception than norm as a much larger number of Gurukuls admitted children based on aptitude of the child irrespective of family background. Students lived in Gurukuls with their teachers, mostly in secluded settings, on 24/7 basis, for several years on exclusive basis. Acceptance to such academies was strict and wards were well screened before admission. Students not having required maturity or lack of sincerity were either refused entry or were kept on a slow pace. Teachers were basically priests, monks, yogis or acclaimed gurus and in due course acquired full knowledge about their families, orientations, social standing and such other critical issue important for development of the self of their disciples. Those matured teachers knew tiniest nuances of their students much ahead of student himself. Just imagine the situation today and conclude how much help to expect from teachers available on hourly rates.

Teachers also play crucial role in shaping value system of their wards. A teacher who treats boys and girls at par in terms of respect and equality, strengthens the capacity of his students to understand human relationships in a better perspective, especially if the child comes from a family where gender equality is not practiced. Similarly, a teacher acting stingy while awarding stars for only exceptional performance, is sending the signal to his wards that success is difficult to come by but its fruits too are rare and worth attempting. Also, as against parents, a teacher is in better and neutral position to identify special talent of his ward in sports, music, painting or some such fields.

It is seen that parents are generally biased or limited in their understanding of allied talents. In contrast, a teacher is better equipped to spot presence of unique talents in a particular ward and to motivate him to pursue those hidden talents with desired commitment. There are examples after examples of teachers spotting such treasures and helping their students in realizing their full potential. A teacher also got power to help the child to accept his negative self-concept, and successfully overcome the same. There are cases where a teacher held his confidence in potential of a child rather relentlessly and ultimately the child turned corners and made great strides as a man with oozing self-esteem. Such examples are real life saver at times.

Role of parents continues to be critical even at school stage of their children. Fine that they have to help in their assignments but more important is to motivate the child to take his schooling as an exciting and learning journey. Parents continuing guidance in matters like time management and balancing recreation and study time, continues all through their schooling. They should stop looking at progress of their ward in terms of external achievements alone. While external achievements are important, but they are not ends by themselves. Achievements are culmination of a long process of coming together of capabilities, skills and hard work of a student. But the ground for all those traits to shine rests on the foundation provided by virtues embedded in self-concept, self-esteem, and self-confidence. Ignoring the foundation always carry risk of stability and safety of the structures constructed above. Parents and teachers must know well that the root of self-esteem of a child is not founded in his academic achievements alone, but those internally generated practices that, among other things, make it possible for him to achieve all the self-virtues required to step into a happy and prosperous future.

In the dream situation the school and teachers should also be able to teach their students how to manage their anger without getting hurt. Also, that throwing tantrums is mostly ineffective and nothing but waste of their own energy. Children also need be told about ways to channelize their excitement as well as impatience. Teachers should must teach them to face their sexual feelings gracefully, with proper acceptance and by avoiding all sorts of self-destructive behaviors. An ideal school will also help children recognize their emotional outbursts without losing their mind or losing their sleep over it. Children from such a school cannot fail in living a happy and satisfied life both on personal level and as part of society at large.

Such ideal teachers shall be guided exclusively by their genuine desire to share their knowledge and experience and not for lure of money or fame. Ideal teacher for boosting the entire concept of self of his student will be showing qualities of calmness, kindness, patience and compassion. She must exhibit living life with humility, sympathy, truthfulness and openness. She must have par excellence record of ethical and moral conduct. Well, it certainly cannot be helped that search of such eligible teachers for enhancing all aspects of self of her students sounds more like daydreaming than a genuine possibility.

3. Role of Society and Communities

Society and communities also play a big role in shaping different aspects of Self in both positive and negative manners. Society surrounds us from all directions. Our relatives, neighbors, opinion makers, policy makers, sports idols, heroes, stars, media, opponents and even strangers on road, individually and collectively come together to form the social and community circles we live in and impact our concept of self in more ways than we can imagine. Society set rules and standards of what is generally perceived as beautiful, excellent, appreciable or ideal, worth following by all others. Society shapes what is fashionable and trendy. It defines gender roles and duties to be discharged by every role player. Concepts of being morally right, politically correct, ethically flawless and religiously tolerable, also are nothing but reflection of collective conscience of our society itself. To ignore the society or get insulated against it, becomes next to impossible for any of its members. That is why, society always get considered as a powerful and influential force.

Speaking frankly, however, society is generally cruel, unforgiving and messed up in many ways. As such, more than its positive impact, social and communal factors got power to inject negativity in an individual's formation of self. People are seen struggling all the time to adhere to norms set by their society and communities. The burden of arranging dowry by the girl's family at her marriage in most part of India is a case in point. The evils associated with illogical diktats by 'khap panchayats' in Haryana or Uttar Pradesh or caste supremacy are yet another burning example of society forcing wrong notions on its young members impacting their personal orientation and coping with what is expected from them.

It is not that only Eastern societies need to bear the burden of this menace. West is equally at fault out here. For decades now, Barbie doll has been presented as ultimate beautiful girl in the West. Millions of girls have been motivated, and even emotionally blackmailed, by mothers to idolize Barbie and control their diet and dressing to get the same body proportions. Researches have established that Barbie lower self-esteem for most young girls and induce increased desires to look skinnier. It has negative influences on body image and causes lower body satisfaction levels among young girls, by giving children false pretenses and pressures about being skinny and perfect. Just imagine that Barbie as a toy was invented in 1959 to allow girls to dream and play out their futures. In due course, Barbie turned out to become aspirational in character and a vehicle for self-expression and storytelling, and ultimately, a true reflection of Western culture.

Interestingly, if Barbie was proportioned to be an actual girl, she would be 5'9" tall, will weigh about 50 kg, will have waist of 18", bust of 39" and hips of 33". Her BMI will be at 16 and she will wear children shoe size 5. Come and think seriously, the body of such a girl could not even accommodate indispensable body organs within it. Forget about giving birth to a child, her neck cannot support her head. Basically, she can never function as a normal girl. In spite of all these anomalies, entire Western society has accepted Barbie as ideal and injected inferiority complex among millions of girls for no rhyme or reason.

Similarly, boys in many places today are made to think that ideal male body is tall, well built, muscular and neither short nor overweight. Gyms are overflowing with herds of boys struggling with instructors, consuming protein shakes to get desired body types. No matter how hard they try in real life, majority of them are never going to get those type of bodies. Thinking loudly, barring sports persons, what benefits accrue from chiseled bodies? Societal pressure has changed the concept of healthy body from disease free and full of energy to a completely artificial look. People make it big when they are motivated by their loved ones, when they work harder and not when their body looks good. Society itself would have been benefited if all those hours spent in gyms were deployed towards social work, community activities, sports or such other extracurricular activities.

Unfortunately, teenagers are the worst target of social pressures. In their impressionable age, they worry peer perceptions just too much. For them, the looks and acceptance become increasingly important even at the cost of academic score or co-curriculum activities. Here again, girls are far more impacted than boys. As per one survey conducted worldwide with a very large sample survey having participants from across fifty nations, seven out of ten girls between the age of 15 to 17 thought they do not measure up to their expectations on three major criteria of looks, school performance and relationships. This was a self-assessment activity with no role from the questioner. Imagine if 70% teenager girls are having low self-esteem on three endearing attributes, how harmful this pressure is for girls.

Unfortunately, this problem does not stop at any age group. Even matured adults are seen struggling on so many counts under social pressure. Businesses enjoy these fears and spend billions to build up and strengthen the stereotypes just to make money. Take the case of TV ads in India. Commercial ads on TV are window of information about the world. Ads are powerful and should mean right things. They appear for few seconds but leave long lasting impressions on the psyche of viewers. Indian ads are notoriously ill famous for objectifying women in general. Women get about 60% of screen time and 56% of talk time but most of this time, women are shown selling beauty products, working in kitchen, cleaning, shopping or frowning over their partners. Women are shown mostly married or desiring to get married with a dependent status. While men are shown as brand ambassadors, women are depicted as brand commodities. In case of women, the focus is clearly on looks and not messaging. So much emphasis goes on skin color and tone that girls with darker shades are under lifelong stress regarding their skin, a thing that has cultural heritage in the background. They are shown nine times stunningly beautiful or attractive, six times in revealing costumes, five times sexually objectified, and four times partially nude (as per a UNICEF study shown on WION TV in April, 2021). A society establishing such regressive trends is perceptualizing the plight of women across generations.

People trying to meet society standards keep doing all the unwanted things all their life. But is such sacrifice worth all the efforts involved? People under pressure from social standards do not see, hear, act, feel, or think from their authentic self. Everything they do is dictated by whether it can earn them social recognition or save them from social criticism. In the end, they have spent their lives following wishes of unknown others and never lived a life of their own. How different this can be from the life of a slave or a prisoner?

4. Role of Cultural Landscapes

Cultural landscapes influence behavior and belief characteristics of a particular society, community or ethnic group. Cultural systems dictate how a person see himself and interprets experiences of interactions with others. Defined standards shaped by our cultural landscape guide emergence of self-perceptions which, in turn, make us look at entire world in a particular way. Our relationship at society at large, our take on morality, our choice of lifestyles, health, food, dressing, community engagement, political preferences are all directly influenced by our cultural backdrop. That is why people living in different parts of the world interpret global issues in starkly different contexts. A person's take whether he likes being independent, different from others, interdependent, self-dependent, expressive in communication, selfish, benevolent or aggressive, entirely depend on his own self-concept that get deeply influenced by the cultural landscape he belongs to. Cultures are also known to make a man comfortable with different experiences felt by individuals. Cultural perspectives also provide insights into psychological processes involved in entire thinking process of a person. Experiences we go through and their inferences on us are directly shaped by the culture we live in. In that sense, culture has even greater role in forming of our self than our parents and family, more so because behavior of parents with their child is also dictated by that very culture to begin with.

Every culture has its own folklore traditions covering their own tales, proverbs, superstitions, riddles, customs, beliefs, forms, rituals, celebrations, festivals, weddings, metaphors, legends, lullabies and myths. In their innumerable variations, all these folklore elements influence learning, practicing skill and most importantly, formation of world view for its audience. Folklore also forms the basis for acceptable moral values of the society concerned. Also, folklore play a role in controlling social behavior amidst the rapidly changing dynamics of the social world. Different narratives presented by folklores find place in deeper consciousness of its audience from early days itself. Above elements cannot but leave their impressions on a person's self-representation. Our tales are spun, but for most part we do not spin them, they spin us. That is how self-image of every person is conditioned by the culture he grows in.

One of the most discussed stereotypes about culture is its division as Western and Eastern. It has been discussed for long that Western culture promotes and rewards individuality, being different from others, self-dependence and self-expressive individuals. While people from East believe in collectivism, inter-dependence, social-centering, being cohesive, and displaying respectful behaviors towards others, especially those seniors in age, social status, profession or position. But this is too simplistic a classification and is like saying that everything under the sun is either white or black. Such a generalization demonstrate disregard for kaleidoscope of global cultural diversity. People coming from different cultures have varying degree of intensity of each individual factor where a wholesome individual emerges out with his uniqueness intact.

On the other hand, there is another set of cultural practices which have zero impact on self formation of a person. Different practices like driving vehicle on left of the road or right, eating with fork spoon or chopsticks or directly with fingers, manner in which one greets others on the road, the way people dress, the languages spoken, the roles assigned to genders, or some such obvious difference, may appear as big gaps on the face of it but are just not important at all for their impact on formation of self. These are just practices having some influence on human psychology and creating some apparent splits diluting unity of humankind than ethnic divergences in mind but nothing beyond.

Culture is not linked to individual's self-perception as directly as generally assumed. The feeling of being dependent or independent impact each person in varying proportion as per context involved. For example, we find individuals from every culture displaying varying sense of involvement in romantic relationships ranging from voluntary, one-sided to being duty bound. Similarly, you come across people from every corner of the world displaying human values of humility, politeness, and mutual respect. Dealing with feelings and emotions in public or privacy are also seen world over.

At the end of the day every culture value a good person. You should have better control over your life situations, should be attending to your duties, should contribute towards good of others and should play your part as per your social status. These are some such expectations that are common among all cultures. It is just that normal assumptions about what it means to be a good person vary from culture to culture. But internalization of all those values is purely an individual trait and that is what is important for development and growth of self.

5. Role of Religions and Heritage

Some people look at religions as a panacea, a source of universal cure of all ailments. Earlier belief held by sociologists that different aspects of religions practiced by families have power to complement as well as motivate self-development, no longer holds ground as recent studies conducted fail to identify any direct role of religions in the formation or growth of self related issues. Self-development starts at an early age of the child by which time religion, even when practiced by parents with full zeal, does not impact a child that much. But aspects of religious practices have indirect impact through actions of parents, and in that sense the impact is rather obstructive and undermining.

But impact of religion becomes stronger on teenagers as religion starts impacting their beliefs and feelings of self-worth. The perceptions of being a child of God, insights into the purpose of life, the promise of forgiveness of sins, the hope of eternal life, as well as involvement in a caring organization may strengthen self-worth. Little later, while the person reaches his adolescence, that crucial age between childhood and adulthood when young people seek independence from parents and family despite not yet knowing who they really are, religious practices start negatively affecting their self-esteem. Feelings of self-worth are especially important during college years when adolescents make critical decisions about education, career, and relationships. Their inevitable indulgence in responding to peer pressures, use of alcohol and substances, experiment with sex, and so on, also attract exasperation as a violation of ways preached by their religious sermons.

The results of some studies, however, demonstrate that positivity of self-concept is partially related between religious belief and psychological adjustment. Consensus among people working in the field however conclude that religious belief had a small, positive, direct effect on adjustment but a larger and negative indirect effect through lesser logical measures associated with religious attributes interfering in control and punishment diktats. Secondly, young people mostly feel frustrated for not being able to easily translate their beliefs into their daily behavior. The hypocrisy of wide gaps between religious preaching and society's actual practices, surely adds to their sense of confusions and dismay.

6. Role of Socio-economic Factors

Impact of socio-economic position on emergence of self-concept has some interesting studies and conclusions. Studies suggest that economic condition of the family has no contribution in self-development of toddlers as the house they live or vehicle they ride does not mean much to them. Love and care of family is all they need. But during the important stage of adolescence children develop awareness of differences between haves and have-nots. At this stage of life, children coming from less affluent backgrounds in particular, suddenly start seeing big gaps when comparing their situation with others on many counts.

So, during transition from childhood to adulthood, young people undergo important changes by variety of other intrapersonal, interpersonal and socio-cultural determinants. That is why adolescence is considered very critical time for the development of lifelong perceptions, beliefs, and values. As it is, adolescents struggle with their developmental tasks of establishing identity, accepting changes in physical characteristics, learning various types of skills, showing interest in hobbies, exploring their sexuality even outside the norms set by their respective family teachings or cultural tradition. Therefore, by the time they are ready to enter adulthood, socio-economic factors start weighing in reshaping or cementing their concepts.

Later, once they are fully into adulthood and start pursuing their occupation, the socio-economic factors gain further impetus for their sense of self. People living in poverty, for sure, take hit on their self-esteem and feel compelled to devalue other aspects of their self as well. Their inability to cater to basic necessities of life for family is taken as failure in life. It is but natural for them to internalize negative and depressing stereotypes that they are poor because they are incompetent and deeply flawed. This low self-esteem does lead to lack of confidence in their own abilities, even if it was intact up until now. Sense of hopelessness, at that stage also looms large.

Ultimately, all factors impacting formation, growth and sustenance of a person's sense of self work simultaneously making an overly complicated matrix. This complex interplay result in unique identity of every adult. At matured stage of a person's life, it become rather impossible to dissect which factor impacted the final personality in lesser or significant manner.

Benefits of Understanding Self

Placement of the section dealing with expected advantages is always a debatable subject. Should it be done after rolling out the entire concept or should it be in the beginning to let the reader become aware of what to expect, always have compelling arguments in favor as well against. For the journey of exploring self, however, rolling out expected advantages in this initial stage is very much a deliberate decision. Exploring self is not some run of the mill self-improvement project but a life changing mission with very transformative impacts. Exploration of self invites the strong hearts who can commit their time, dedication, and will power to pursue this journey over months and years.

That is why listing progressive advantages, at this very stage of this book, is perfectly intentional as exposure to expected benefits is likely to fuel reader's active curiosity and help them have their own cost-benefit estimations. In a way, this section also spans out the likely route plan to help reader make an intelligent inference about things to come. All this is expected to encourage and motivate readers to continue investing their time and energy for learning and exploring about this great expedition.

Interestingly, the very expedition of understanding self is a long-drawn process just like climbing a snow covered peak. Starting with the base camp, the very sight of scenery keeps changing altogether with progressive climb giving glimpses of peculiar features which one may have only read or heard before. In the journey of exploring self also, new findings and experiences begin as soon as one starts marching upwards, offering access to some low hanging fruits in initial days itself. Later, the climb upward, offers varying experiences on daily basis. Understanding Self is literally and figuratively similar to climbing one's own Mount Everest in every sense of the word.

Understanding self improves our interaction with people around in significant manner. We are also helped through improved intellectual perspective bringing better connection with the Universe and positivity filled attitude ensuring better future. In addition, we can be sure to gain sizable benefits at social and psychological levels.

At the later stage of life, benefits of self exploration extend towards detachment from the world of objects and removal of false image of individual self being different than universal self, the supreme purpose of human life (also called Moksha). As per Ancient Indian traditions, the release from the continuing 'cycles of death and rebirth' is considered highest stage of human evolution, and hence, supreme objective of human life. That is why Indian traditions evaluate every human endeavor in terms of its impact on crossing over this illusionary world, and merging of individual being with the Supreme, called by various names. No wonder then Indian culture primarily highlights spiritual benefits of all individual and social initiatives. The same applies for evaluating advantages of Understanding Self.

Spiritual benefits expected from shining Self are comparable to an fully developed and matured Banyan Tree (Bargad). Being very large in size, Banyan tree offers shelters to many beings, its fruits feed the birds, leaf feed many animals, and shade help lot many human beings. While it does not consume ground water itself, it attracts clouds for rains in nearby areas. Even after so much offerings for the betterment of other living beings, Banyan tree can survive up to 400 years. Its aerial prop roots mature into thick woody trunks totally indistinguishable from original trunk. On the same lines, the aura of a person fully aware about his Self, makes use of his wisdom benefiting everyone around without being burden in any way.

Let us now look at a random order of various advantages reported by people who have travelled down this path in the past.

- Improves self-identity, helping in better recognition of one's potential and qualities as an individual, especially in social context.
- Enhances self-knowledge leading to improved chances of all round success by lowering chances of failures.
- Bridges gap between self-perception and perception held by others. This bridging helps in better relationships. One becomes better in every social role including being a father, spouse, friend, work colleague or even a business associate.
- Better understanding of Self results in drastic reduction of doubts and distractions facilitating quicker and well thought out decision making.

- Brings surety in expecting help in bringing positive changes in allied qualities like self-control, self-efficacy, self-determination, self-motivation and self-confidence etc. Increased power, potency, energy and force for all these characteristics results in carving out a better version of our self.
- Adds complete clarity about one's unique strengths and weaknesses. This clarity converts into greater money-making opportunities with lower inputs and higher returns.
- Brings in consistency, stability and sturdiness in our entire thought process bringing positive reflections on our actions and behavior.
- Helps in bringing hidden fears and anxieties out in open. This adds to sense of mental peace boosting creativity, imagination and intuition.
- By being aware of real triggers behind one's emotional responses, the person is helped in dealing with issues based on objectivity and rationality. Improvement in emotional quotient so achieved, contributes in entire gamut of emotional balance including augmenting capacity to perceive, use, understand, manage, and handle emotions within desired swings.
- Brings clarity about person's distinct abilities and skills. As a result, the person gains better guidance to pick up chosen sports, hobbies, vocational studies, academics specialization as well as choice of profession and, of course, with higher chances of progress and success.
- Self-understanding leads to added self-confidence and sense of control over events in life helping people face worst of their times and to perform at full potential.
- Helps in taking right call about own standing with respect to entire surrounding environment. This helps in becoming an effective member at social interactions and seamlessly becoming part of all types of gatherings and congregations.
- Understanding self helps in getting rid of all types of complexes including inferiority and superiority. This enhances ability to avoid getting intimidated by criticism of others.
- Makes people better at discriminating between genuine compliments from others and mere sycophancy, and prepares for accepting appreciation from others with grace.
- Deeper and better understanding about own real self helps in making hopes, dreams and aspirations more realistic adding additional chances of success in whatever activities get pursued in different spheres of life.
- Better understanding and acceptance for self without any shades of deceptions, help in achieving a unique combination of strength, ability and will, which in turn comes out as an effective entity assuring success.
- Clear self-understanding brings in critical components of self-efficacy and self-respect making a person feel comfortable to meet basic challenges thrown by actual life from time to time.
- Deeper understanding of self helps in getting over scars of deficient parenting, lack of finances, social non-acceptance, poor educational opportunities or even personal tragedies of severe nature. These all are otherwise known factors

hampering proper growth of self-esteem or over all self-concept. That way, understanding self creates a unique level playing field for everyone to grow.

- Developed self-understanding reconnects a person with his own authentic self, which becomes useful in perfecting alignment among thoughts, beliefs, actions, skills, abilities, interests, talents, wisdom and insights. Living real life with our own authentic self converts normal life into living in heaven right here, in this very world.
- Helps in exercising control over anxieties, worries and impulses enabling proper appreciation and encashment of opportunities offered by life in general.
- Empowers to fight the feeling of loneliness due to lack of connectedness with loved ones and friends.
- Cultivates optimism and guard against adverse influences of fantasies.
- Helps in avoiding cynicism by making individuals more realistic. It reduces dependence on external conditions for one's own happiness.
- Works as a booster for enhancing self-esteem grounded in self-acceptance by pushing idealism out of the system.
- Improves communication with self as well as others. This leads to better collaboration with one and all.
- Broadens one's ability to comprehend views of others with open mind without being too critical or judgmental.
- Helps in peeling away conditioned psychological aspects generated from subconscious systems.
- Allows better access to higher levels of consciousness.
- Provides access to inner silence and peace by allowing access with one's personal sanctuary of bliss.
- Develops the interconnectedness that all fellow beings are travelers in the same journey called life with by and large similar abilities, ambitions, failings and limitations.
- Aids in realizing that there is a power well above whatever is visible in this physical world and inspires to see direct connect with 'that'.
- Makes a person capable of remaining in the state of heightened awareness for self as well as others.

Self may be seen as the Wise Being within all of us, the energy of our highest potential waiting to be expressed.

"Knowing yourself is the beginning of all wisdom". Aristotle

2

Understanding Peripheral Concepts

Self is very intimate concept and each person has his own take on it in one way or the other. There are things about it that we know and many others that need be learned or refreshed. Side by side, there exist division of a person on internal and external planes. While one's thoughts, desires, behaviors, attitudes and experiences get clubbed as internal aspects, features like name, age, education, position, social standing, interests etc. represent his external existence. Generally, we look at Self from a first person's perspective, but staunch advocates suggest looking at it purely from third person's perspective. Both perspectives are established as valid and imperative to define this complex entity. These factors do have their own limited relevance but do not describe an individual in totality. In any case, these aspects or features exist because of the individual and not the vice versa.

Real self refers to deepest core of a person. Before looking at the real comprehensive Self embedded in the core, let us broadly look at concepts lying on the periphery of this very core. Taking the ancient method of comprehending any gigantic subject, let us dissect each of these known concepts, one by one, understand them in greater detail and retain the part that goes in defining or clarifying the core, and push aside those parts that fail to illuminate the core in any significant way. Many of these aspects sound very familiar but can prove as broken spoke in the wheel. That is why we should be done and dusted with them for our larger objective. Through this time-tested method, at the end of the process, we are sure to be left with only and only the aspects representing basic core.

Key Terms and Concepts in Daily Life

Moving further involves extensive and profound use of some heavy and complex concepts and attributes. These words get often used in daily life but these are not mere words as these represent underlying concepts with very specific connotations applied for comprehending their intrinsic and contextual meaning. Developing clear comprehension and deeper meaning of these key concepts is highly advised to ensure that readers rightly absorb their real meaning only and not their casual reference or limited meaning floating around in common parlance. From now on, every time these words get used in the entire book, the readers are strongly advised to understand their use in intended context only.

Attitude: Is a psychological construct, a settled way of thinking or feeling. It refers to a set of emotions, beliefs and behaviors towards a particular object, person, thing, or event. Attitude evolves life experiences and range from extremely negative to extremely positive. It can even be conflicted. We can also understand it as feelings held by an individual about himself as well as world around. It can also be ranging from concrete to abstract. Attitude hold very powerful influence over behavior of a person. Attitudes are generally enduring over longer times but are not cast in steel and are seen changing when life situations change significantly.

Aptitude: Is an innate inborn ability or capacity to learn to do a job at certain level. Aptitude may be dormant or developed. It can be specific or general. It is different from both skills and abilities. Skills describe what a person has learned to do in the past. Abilities describe what a person can do now while aptitudes, as a forward-looking description, is what a person has the ability to do in the future. Speaking comparatively, one can train aptitude more easily than attitude. Right aptitude also got right influence over attitude.

Behavior: The way in which one acts or conducts himself, especially towards others. Basically, a psychological trait, human behavior is the potential and expressed mental, physical or social capacity of an individual or group to respond to both internal and external sensations. Also driven by thoughts and feelings, it can be objectively observable, introspective or even nonconscious. Behavior is generally objective and can be studied scientifically unlike a normal mental subjective activity. Falling over wide spectrum, behavior of a person may be anything from common, normal, unusual, acceptable to other extremes. Society plays a big role in both forming and interpreting individual behavior.

Belief: Is an unyielding idea that a thing is true. Usually referred about religion, it is based on revelation by a person or text(s). It differs from a scientific knowledge that is open for testing. Being beyond logic or reasoning, it works as a limiting factor in so far as it proves a big obstacle in the way of fresh rational insemination of learning.

Habit: Is formed over time by regular repetition of a certain behavior or tendency. Once formed, it requires little or no thought for repetition and starts to occur voluntarily even subconsciously. Habit can be part of any activity, ranging from eating and sleeping to thinking and reacting. It develops through reinforcement and repetition. Habits can be both good and bad. Habits are not desirable as they are always hard to break. People with habits tend to feel frustrated when their habits do not serve them and they fail to make changes.

Experiences: As a noun, experience means direct observation or participation in an event. It can also mean knowledge, skill or practice derived from direct observation of or participation in an activity or event. In general, experiences are personally encountered, undergone or lived through. But all these meanings are not applied to experiences used all through this book. The true meaning of 'experiences' refers to an event that has been actually lived through and which repeatedly keeps coming back in the conscious space of the person, reminding him of the pleasures, sensations, pains and aversions that was felt at the time when it initially happened. It is different from a scenario that is just imagined or thought about as a possibility. Experiences used here are personal, become part of the person's life, and most importantly, the memory of the experience becomes part of who that individual is.

Memories: Are the entire range of processes that involves ability to both preserve and recall information learned or experienced. It is not, however, a flawless process and mistakes do happen frequently in storing or recalling of the information. Most of memories remain outside conscious space and retrieval process brings them out to conscious awareness when desired. But recall versions are largely situational and differ from time to time, depending on the mental condition at the time of recall. While its processes are not perfect, human beings are capable of remembering astonishingly large volume of data even when it is susceptible to mistakes and errors.

Values: Refer to sense of right and wrong. It refers to appropriate course of action and define what 'ought' to be. For example, trust and affection can be seen foundational values across societies. Values are socially approved desires and goals that are internalized through the process of conditioning, learning and socializing and go to become subjective preferences, standards and aspirations. Values also attach degrees of goodness to all activities and relationships. They remain integral part of one's philosophy of life impacting aims, ideals, manner of thinking and principles by which one's behavior get guided.

Expressions Around Self

Let us now take up some of the better-known characteristics or expressions around Self in order to understand each of these in their right contexts. Having looked at all these in desired depth, we would have removed many ambiguities and confusions from the real concept of Self. Understanding so developed will certainly help us in unravelling some of mysteries surrounding Self.

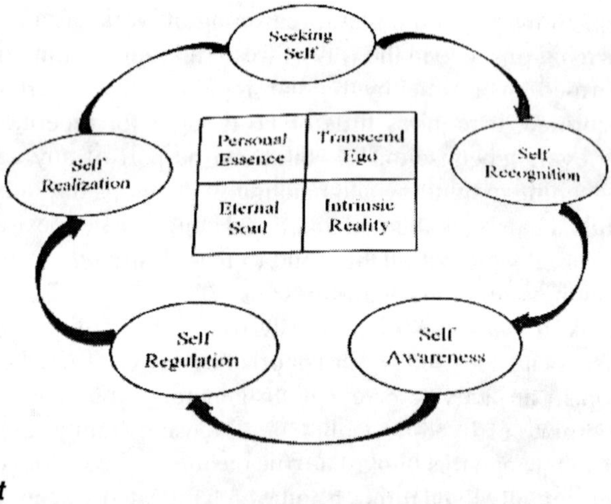

1. Self-Concept

Self-concept or self-identity is conceptual understanding held by people for their own existence. In general, it is the sum of person's knowledge and understanding about himself. In that sense, it is also called 'self-knowledge'. Successes and failures of people in many areas of life gets closely linked to the views they hold about themselves and their relationship with others. This concept emerges very gradually and remains dynamic. It gets shaped and reshaped based on the interactions and perception of experiences with important people around, mainly, parents, family members, teachers and friends.

Self-concept is different from self-consciousness, which is an awareness or preoccupation with oneself. Self-concept largely includes physical, psychological and social components. It is normal to come across people perceiving themselves way different than what others think about them. Such individuals ultimately face many doubts and get inflicted with scars on their thinking process. Individual's own degree of accuracy on his inner self becomes important in this situation to bring clarity in one way or the other.

Self-concept is an umbrella used by social sciences to explain an individual's own understanding about himself as an isolated distinct entity. It does include many other allied concepts dealing with this subject, including but not limited to self-analysis, self-control, self-determination, self-efficacy, self-evaluation, self-knowledge, self-perception, self-monitoring, self-stimulation and self-discipline. Now all these parts or aspects are found in each one of us with varying degree of evolution. What segregates one person from another is how these are held together as a single identity. You come into existence when these parts come together and create the illusion of unique individuality. That is also why our identity is said to be a temporary construct.

In terms of psychology, self-concept refers to conscious and reflective personality of an individual. It does include all the information that a person makes use of while attempting answer to a question "what am I like?" Good comprehension of self-concept is a pre-requisite for manifested self-awareness as well as self-consciousness. Interestingly, self-awareness is also an integral part of the self-concept and to that extent these concepts are overlapping.

Since self-concept gets evolved very gradually, it tends to be consistent, stable and strong. Studies suggest that people generally behave in line with their self-concept irrespective of the impact on outcomes being positive, neutral or adverse. These qualities of self-concept pose problems while bringing in changes desired at attitudes and behavior levels. However, the fact that self-concept evolves and is not entirely instinctively in nature, it offers boundless potential for its positive development and advancement. A little bit of change in any single part or little bit of dilution in any earlier understanding, leads to change of the earlier identity into a newer you. Later when one start using Meditation and introspection or other tools and techniques, there comes the realization that our identity or individuality exists as a sum of many of these parts and not in any specific part/aspect. This realization helps in sinking of new understanding that it is not static as we had been believing it to be.

According to Carl Rogers, one of the founders of humanistic psychology, self-concept consists of three distinct components of self-image, self-esteem and ideal self. According to his views, self-image is largely the physical entity like brown hair, blue eyes, tall and our social roles of being a spouse, brother, or a teacher and our personality traits like being outgoing, serious, or kind. Self-image doesn't always match reality as people are seen holding inflated perception of one or more of their characteristics. These inflated perceptions may be positive or negative, and an individual may simultaneously hold a more positive view of certain aspects of his self and a more negative view of others.

Self-esteem is an independent concept and is being taken separately. Lastly, the ideal self, as the name suggests, is what we actually desire to be. Often, we find difference between one's self-image and his own ideal self. As per Carl Rogers, self-image and ideal self can both be congruent or incongruent. They are called congruent when there is a fair amount of overlap between the two, a very desirable situation. Conversely, incongruence between these two leads to undesirable internal confusion that stands in the way of deeper exploration of self. Such incongruity also impacts one's self-esteem negatively.

2. Self-Confidence

Self-confidence is yet another critical concept considered a logical extension of self itself. While it does reflect on some aspects of self it fails to explain the same in any significant way. Basically, self-confidence is an attitude about one's skills and abilities. It is a sort of self-assurance in our own judgment, thinking and views. Higher self-confidence can also be called an assertion of belief that initiatives, to be initiated in due course, stand good chance of being accomplished. Self-confidence brings direct effect on our interest, enthusiasm and self-regulation and thus influences actual achievements in real life.

In a way, positive self-confidence spreads a sense of control over events in life. While it need not be compared with motivation, it plays as a factor in what we perceive we can perform. Interestingly, self-confidence does play big role towards the level of dedication applied in achieving desired results. In that sense, self-confidence also stands apart from concept of self-esteem which relates to admiration or respect given by someone to his own perception of his qualities.

A self-confident person carry ability to correctly judge his own social and personal standing. Being a very likable trait, people in the surrounding environment end up admiring a self-confident person as he is at ease with self, work, situations and people alike. This attitude feeds trust and positivity. Always doing what he believes in, willing to take risks, admitting to mistakes, accepting compliments graciously, not getting intimidated by criticism from others, are all sure signs of a self-confident person.

Speaking conversely, a person low on self-confidence is surrounded by self-doubts; he tends to be submissive, passive and shows lack of trust in his own abilities as well in others. Less confident person is prone to inferiority complex and feels unloved, less cared and extra sensitive to criticism from every quarter. The concept of self-confidence is much more important for students as it has direct cause and effect on their academic performance. At school level, self-confidence or lack of it has direct bearing on ensuring academic success. Besides grades, it also deters ill effects of bullying and harassments which, unfortunately, have become part of schooling days all over the world. Lack of self-confidence brings down self-esteem of the student and turns out a very demotivating factor for learning. As such, building right confidence is the greatest help parents, family and teachers provide to the young ones in their formative years.

Suggestions for boosting Self-Confidence

Gaining clarity about your value system goes a long way in improving self-confidence. The sense of importance about a thing, how to behave in each situation, how to respond within family or among friends or what is generally appropriate are all issues linked with our values. Working within the cherished values go to boost the confidence and vice versa. Values dictate if a particular habit or behavior is acceptable or otherwise. The rules we decide to live by, or goals we set for achieving or ideals we set for ourself, are all linked to values, and working within boundaries of those very values makes us feel confident.

Usual suspects for lower self-confidence are excessive expectations, harsh self-judgement, preoccupation with fear, lack of experience, and lack of skill. Accordingly, many of the suggestions available for boosting it, revolve around building safeguards against these negative impacts. Let us briefly list out those and some other practical ways to take care of self-confidence.

- Become an optimist because a pessimist only sees difficulties in every opportunity coming his way. We have no right to expect anything other than best possible outcome under any situation. Afterall, there is always a solution to every problem.
- Stop comparing yourself with others. Rarely, you may know enough about others to make fair comparisons. As we are slowly learning, knowing about own self itself involves so many complications, how can we be sure about others? In general, people are good at counting other's blessing and own miseries. It is normal to overlook handicaps of others. Best is to compare you with your previous avatar.
- Surround with positive people because people filled with negativity can belittle your ambitions in no time. A person low on positivity can at best lead a mediocre life, period. Be selective in people allowed to operate within your personal circle at all times.
- Communicate freely with the external world. Let it be about your feelings, emotions, thoughts, desires or whatever. Quality communication brings added clarity and leads to better understanding about each other and provide a good boost to your own level of confidence.
- Take care of physical and mental health as confidence is best founded on strength. People basing their confidence on thin air can be seen falling flat.
- Be kind to yourself because nobody cares for you as much you do yourself. Neither anyone else knows your strengths and weaknesses as good as yourself. Judging yourself too harshly carry the risk of errors in thinking.
- Practice positive self-talks as many people report good results of this practice. You must love, trust and respect yourself and feel good about who you are. Positive self-talks also impress others. It is always nice to feel good about yourself.
- Face your fears directly and squarely. When you attempt doing what you initially thought you cannot do, you gain enormous confidence even if you fail. Not trying is said to be the worst of all options on most occasions.
- Focus on tomorrow and not yesterday. Why should you pity yourself even if you grew with lesser support, unfavorable environment or imperfect surroundings? One can read about all successful people, dead or alive, none of them allowed their past to come in their way of growing. Success is founded on today and is built on tomorrow.

3. Self-Esteem

Self-esteem refers to admiration and respect being given by an individual to himself. Among all other aspects of Self explained here, Self-esteem impacts our daily life on wider scale and hence should be interesting to study for multiple benefits. Self-esteem is made up of our view of all the things that define us as a person including our personality, accomplishments, talents, capabilities, backgrounds, experiences, relationships and special connections. It is the picture we paint about our self except that this picture is painted with colors of perceptions and not of reality; the question is not what we are but what we think we are.

Consisting of the critical components of self-efficacy and self-respect, self-esteem is about a person's self-assessment as being competent to meet basic challenges of life, and worthy of happiness. Characteristics of self-efficacy comprises of all factors boosting confidence in one's ability to think, learn, choose, and make appropriate decisions. Similarly, characteristics of positive self-respect reassure that one is worthy to receive love, friendship, achievement, success. Also, that these blessings are natural and appropriate, and most importantly, the person receiving them deserves them well. Self-esteem comes out important as it has capacity to undermine all other positive traits or qualities of the person.

A person having low self-esteem lacks fundamental self-trust or confidence irrespective of what other valuable assets he has. The same would be true if a person lacks a basic sense of self-respect, feels unworthy of the love or respect of others, or feels undeserving of happiness. Low self-esteem injects fear in the mind of the person limiting his ability to assert thoughts, wants, or needs alike.

Self-esteem is believing in your capabilities to learn, achieve, contribute, extending help, and autonomy to operate without interference. High self-esteem magnifies the sense of person's ideas, feelings and opinions. Self-esteem is not the euphoria or buoyancy that may be temporarily induced by a drug, a compliment, or a love affair. Self-esteem is always grounded and has nothing to do with momentary delusions in someone's consciousness. Self-esteem necessarily gets build over time and remains intact only when the person lives normal life consciously, responsibly, and with integrity.

Supportive upbringing during childhood kick off the process of formation of self-esteem. That is why a child must be understood and supported in terms of his needs, and feelings. Adults around must support and value children's ideas and contributions to help their self-esteem initiate on strong footings. Also critical is to offer a child with positive thinking heredity. Later when schooling starts, self-esteem get significantly impacted by academic achievements. Higher scores are good quantitative measurements for identifying positive difference from fellow students and work well for comparisons within a heterogeneous group.

Outcome of such comparisons are bound to influence positive as well as negative feelings among young and old alike. During adolescence, peer influence becomes dominating force for self-esteem building. Having several close friends goes a long way in having self-esteem of desired quality. Friends normally do not look down each other as aggressively as strangers and even if there exist differences among friends, the same do not pinch so much as differences with non-friends. Rejections, humiliations and intimidations from peers pull esteem down immediately and sow seeds of self-doubts.

Personal outlook and feedback from peers are other important factors helping growth of self-esteem in positive territory. Life impacting events like death in the family, traumatic accidents, divorce between parents, domestic violence, are other incidents having power to pull down self-esteem of a young mind. Young adults also get impacted more by skills at sports, looks, attraction shown by opposite sex friends. Similarly, the matured adults get impacted more by titles, flashy material possessions, holiday destinations and fashion standings. Self-esteem plateau by the time a person reaches his middle age years. Later, in old age, it starts declining as the matured aged person develops wider acceptance for differences with others on many counts. For example, for a person in his late sixties, the issues impacting self-esteem converts to health condition, cognitive ability and socio-economic status. Other common factors known to have either positive or negative influence can be summarized as racial cordiality, gender neutral respect, neglect, poverty, and social acceptance.

As already mentioned, self-esteem can move from high to low or vice versa. Interestingly, if a person has high self-esteem for a given live issue, at any given point of time, it doesn't mean that self-esteem will be higher for other issues as well. Also, self-esteem is not always black or white. There can always remain a grey area in between. As a result, it is quite possible that one single person maintains high self-esteem for some of his parts and low self-esteem for others. So, the best way is to look at sum of self-esteem and consider it as high when total of positives are more than negatives. The bottom line remains that high self-esteem allows you to celebrate your strengths, challenges and even shortcomings while low esteem enhances your weak spots and pulls down worth of even your prized assets.

Why Does Self-esteem Matters

Self-esteem matters so much because it heavily influences a person's choices and decisions. It affects virtually every facet of life including physical health, effectiveness at work and in all types of relationships. Self-esteem impacts as a motivational factor thereby influencing people in exploring their full potential. Let us briefly look at other interesting areas where higher self-esteem makes substantial impact:

- It is key to mental health and wellbeing
- It provides strength to handle adversity.
- It removes the need of keeping undue focus on some issues.
- It protects against self-blame, self-doubts, helplessness for things that you lack or are not happy about.
- It pulls you out of forces having negative feelings.
- It fuels prosocial behavior like generosity, philanthropy and generally contribute to better human relations.
- It works as a high-level source of motivation to accomplish goals.
- It helps you have better control over your actions.
- It helps in shaking off unfavorable events or negative judgments directed by others.

Self-esteem should not be confused with arrogance neither it makes one egoistical or infallible. Self-esteem also differs from self-confidence which impacts belief about one's ability to do things successfully whereas self-esteem is just about admiration or respect perceived in abilities or lack thereof. So, while one is quality per se, the other is the perceived assessment about that very quality. However, both self-confidence and self-esteem do have intrinsic characteristics having good visibility in terms of body language, down or up shoulders and the way eye contact is made with others.

Patterns Eroding Self-Esteem

There are some distinct patterns that have eroding impact on Self-esteem. It is certainly helpful to look at them to safeguard against. First of all, there is a common syndrome of 'All-or-nothing'. This applies to looking at things in extremes. It is wrong to consider a thing either too good or too bad. Something going wrong is not an indication of worst possible results. Under this influence, a person feels like "if I am unable to do this job well, I will be a total failure." Next pattern is remaining engaged in Mental Filtering, a condition of remaining busy in dwelling only on the negative outcomes in daily life. A simple mistake is enough for such person to ignite unending thinking process that he is not good for any thing in life.

Next pattern is about habit of even converting positives into negatives. Under this influence, a person tends to reject the dimensions of his positive achievements and believes only in negative side of the outcome. For example, when such a person gets good score at annual exams, he concludes that the paper was too easy. Similarly, when he gets hired by a reputed MNC, he thinks that the company must be in hurry to fill the vacancy else he stood no chance to get in. Yet another pattern eroding self-esteem is remaining busy in negative self-talks. Self-talks have life altering impacts. One can change his circumstances through positive self-talks. Negative self-talks, on the other hand, reinforce negative beliefs much faster than positive self-talks fueling positivity. What you talk constantly to yourself converts into your inner voice. And what you tell yourself is what you are likely to tell others through subtle behaviors.

How to Cultivate High Self-Esteem

The good news is that self-esteem is open for correction, but the bad news is that it takes efforts, determination, and great amount of willingness to do that. The process involves examining and countering negative self-image formed over years and years of actual circumstances and experiences. One is required to learn to give grace to himself, something that sounds very easy but is very difficult to practice. Basically, all initiatives focused on building higher self-esteem begin with establishing close friendship with oneself. You must be willing to gloss over your flaws as a friend and should be able to see mirror of reality to avoid the influence of negative views and attitudes. This exercise calls for advancing your spiritual compass where humility to accept compliments and seeking support wherever required can co-exist with love with oneself remaining intact. This life transforming deeper understanding of Self is scheduled for detailed explanation in later part of this book.

4. Individual's Personality

Personality, according to Encyclopedia of Psychology, refers to individual differences in characteristic patterns of thinking, feeling and behaving. The study of personality focuses on two broad areas: understanding individual differences in particular personality characteristics, such as sociability and understanding how various parts of a person come together as a whole. The very word of Personality evolved from Latin word Persona meaning the mask worn by performers in theatrical performances. This mask allows them to perform different roles and help actors disguise their real identity from the spectators in front. The intelligent people have been busy philosophizing personality since antiquity because humanity was always interested in anticipating how to predict why people do what they do. Understanding the rationale or logic behind actions by others enhances our capability to expect their reactions and be ready to protect against their consequences.

Each person has an idiosyncratic pattern of enduring, long-term characteristics and a way to interact with other individuals and the world around them. Personality is considered long term, stable, and not easily changeable. For long, size of human skull and its protrusion in four different sides was used to indicate individual's basket of traits. But our discussions about personality are linked with its more recent evolution as a branch of science called as Personality Psychology. Sigmund Freud, the Austrian neurologist, philosopher and the founder of psychoanalysis, born in 1856, is credited for inventing and developing the technique of psychoanalysis. Sigmund came out with a clinical method for treating psychopathology through dialogue between a patient and a psychoanalyst and also proposed that personality was made of three distinct elements, namely Id, Ego and Superego (Interested readers may like to study this theory of their own in desired details).

Most popular theory of personality traits is called the 'Big Five Theory of OCEAN', five broad traits that an individual can be rated higher or lower when compared to other people, based on the extent to which the person exhibits them, namely, Openness, Conscientiousness, Extroversion, Agreeableness, and Neuroticism. Under this theory, besides these main five group traits, their narrower personality facets are also used to evaluate a person. As such, Openness also makes use of allied traits of openness-to-experience and open-mindedness and roughly reflects as to how receptive a person is to new ideas. Intellectual curiosity and creative imagination are also covered as part of being open. The category under Consciousness includes person's tendency to control impulses and act with responsibility, for example, keeping things in order, dependability at work, and punctuality. Extroversion represents the level of energy with which a person interacts with other people and include being social and assertive. Agreeableness is a person's degree of positivity and helpfulness toward other people and include respectfulness toward others, compassion, and trusting others. Finally, Neuroticism refers to being emotionally stable and the way he experiences challenging emotional states like anxiety and depression.

There are multiple explanations about evolution of personality. Parents and immediate family are obviously considered as the initial building block for its evolution. Proponents of this idea believed that different styles of attachments experienced by a child give rise to their being trusting, social, and confident in day-to-day life. Later theories gave larger credit to peer pressures as primary influencer of the personality and behavior patterns during their adulthood. Many other theories, on the other hand, establish connection of personality traits with impact from life experiences.

In conclusions, however, there seems to be agreement that personality characteristics are both inherent and acquired, remain malleable with the environmental influences, and hence offer opportunity to bring desired changes, provided however, the owner takes up the big challenges of removing that mask and face his own reality. Finally, all personality traits also are just a subset of an individual and do not define him in any comprehensive manner. Personality traits have off late been used by businesses with the assumption that better understanding of traits of their target consumers will help in better targeting product promotions through advertisements etc. for larger reach. Besides, the theory of traits seems more of a logical extension of the Self-Concept already explained.

Many people draw a direct correlation between self and personality but that can never be true. If self is called as a person's core, his personality is just a manifestation of that core, and that too without factoring many ifs and buts.

5. Self-Consciousness

Self-consciousness is a heightened sense of awareness of oneself. It is not to be confused with consciousness which is awareness of internal and external existence. In the contemporary sense of the term, self-consciousness is a preoccupation with oneself, especially with how others might perceive one's appearance or one's actions. When we are self-conscious, it feels like we are on stage and every movement or every step is being scrutinized by the audience. Beyond a limit, being excessively conscious of one's appearance or manner converts into a problem. Such self-consciousness is often associated with shyness or feeling of embarrassment which in turn results into lack of pride and low self-esteem. However, on the positive side, during periods of high self-consciousness, we know our self in an objective manner.

Being self-conscious can be divided into two distinct categories of private and public self-consciousness. In case of private self-consciousness, a person goes into introspection mode to explore his feelings and impressions. Public self-consciousness, on the other hand, refers to awareness of self as viewed by others. It occurs when being observed, or judged. This is the unwanted part of being self-conscious as it generates social anxiety. Under impact of public self-consciousness, person's entire focus of attention shifts from outside to his own self making him become self-conscious of every thought and every action. A public self-conscious person is consumed with thoughts of wondering what the other person(s) are thinking about him. Being excessively self-conscious affect behavior and quite negatively. People suffering from this syndrome are also more likely to suffer from increased stress and anxiety. So, self-consciousness is running away from self rather than coming closer and represents that ugly part of the whole which is quite insignificant but quite obvious and visible, which appears much bigger than its reality.

6. Sense of Self-Awareness

Being self-aware is all about having a better knowledge and comprehension of yourself. This includes being aware about your feelings and character. If you are a self-aware person, you stand much better chance to learn why you feel the way you feel or why do you behave in a manner that you actually behave. Developed sense of self-awareness provides opportunity and freedom to bring required changes within one's thinking and behavior. It's almost impossible to change and become self-accepting if you are unsure as to who you are. Having clarity about who you are and what you want is empowering, giving you the confidence to make changes.

Self-awareness may include different aspects of the self, such as, feelings, qualities, and desires. Self-awareness is often considered a positive quality. Being better aware about self equips every person to become better part of society and function well towards forming and maintaining relationships. A self-aware person is supposed to have learned the working of his mind in terms of thinking, feeling and behaving. Mindfulness, the simple art of fully attending to what is happening, what one is doing or remaining aware about the space one is moving through, is just another aspect of self-awareness itself.

Self-awareness is having a clear perception of your characteristics including strengths, weaknesses, thoughts, beliefs, and emotions. Self-awareness also allows you to understand other people, how they perceive you, your attitude and your responses to them at any given moment. Self-awareness is the first step in creating what you want, where you focus your attention, your emotions, reactions, and behaviors. A self-aware person is better equipped to develop growth mindset as he is able to learn from his mistakes, makes better use of opportunities coming his way. Such a person crosses over his challenges by making better use of things he is good at. Self-awareness also enables self-reflections and self-monitoring resulting in better learnings from failures and thereby ensuring definite success in later efforts.

Self-awareness is a matter of great importance for our basic purpose of 'Understanding Self', hence, this will be taken as full-fledged topic for detailed understanding at a later stage.

7. Authentic Self

Multiple aspects covered in previous sections represent some of the parts of what we are in bits and pieces. There is yet another aspect that comes out much more critical in terms of representing our entire existence called authentic self, an aspect where what you say aligns perfectly with what you think and what you do; where there is no gap between what you think and believe and how you show the same to external world or how you act. This aspect is termed as 'authentic' because it is entirely different than the opposite situation which can be described as fictional self, where the story line is based on what it should be rather than being embedded in reality.

Authentic self is beyond what you think you are or how others look at you. It has also nothing to do with your background, education, work or any such other feature generally used to describe you. Authentic self is also totally independent of your worth in terms of bank balances, self-assessments or statements of others. Authentic self operates on your deepest core level much beyond visible or quantifiable qualities. Also, the focus of all your thoughts, words and deeds remains centered on your own self with no impact of what other people, including people in very close circle (spouse, children and friends included) might say, think or get impacted about. A person operating from his authentic self does nothing under influence of 'people pleasing' tactics including following social norms just because they happen to be socially accepted, culturally approved or politically correct.

Authentic self is also entirely different from being your 'Best Self'. Best self is a fabricated/decorated costume used for specific moments or occasions. Best self is like pictures posted on social platforms where lots of augmentation are applied to show only the best aspects by cropping off all unwanted aspects. Best self is more like a façade, a temporary mask used while on stage. Your authentic self is your unedited version, your original selfie without photoshop and devoid of applying filters of all types.

Most importantly, authentic self is directly connected with happiness index of the owner because such a person always remains perfectly at ease with firm belief of sufficiency; that there are no inadequacies; that one is enough with whatever is available. Since the person here remains true to his own sense of values, his actions thoughts or words do not generate any stress or pressure ensuring his happiness and bliss remaining intact. Reconnecting to authentic self happens when you put your life together in a way that you start respecting yourself just the way you are, what you have and what you do. Life of a person embedded with his authentic self keeps flowing with energy and excitement. He enjoys calm mental state and feels and enjoys both silence and happiness at the same time. The person here completely trust himself and just disregards or remains apathetic towards both likes or dislikes of others.

Here is a quick test to see which self is running your life, authentic self or fictional self? In the following lines, on the vertical scale, there are some questions representing real life scenarios applicable to a normal person. On the horizontal scale, there are five different possibilities of ranging from one extreme to another as given below:

a.	True all the time	Possible score 5
b.	True most of the time	Possible score 4
c.	True only sometimes	Possible score 3
d.	Mostly Untrue	Possible score 2
e.	Entirely Untrue	Possible score 1

Now you are going to test your own score as to how much you are being governed by your authentic self so there is a reason to be completely true with your answers. All you need to do is ensure your full privacy, a quite space and an active mind and, of course, a pencil to help you write each score. In case you do not identify with the questions, you may feel free to replace any one of the following questions with something similar and applicable to your individual situation. Please take sufficient time with each question and recollect couple of real-life examples you have gone through before coming up with your reply.

Scorecard for testing your degree of living as Authentic Self
Test Designed for checking Degree of Authentic Self Living

1 I do make efforts to please seniors/elders to draw their attention and approval towards my actions and accomplishments.
2 Opinion of others remain in foreground of my own esteem assessments pushing my internal value system in background.

3 I do hesitate to work of my own sweet will and many of my initiatives are governed by fear of disapproval from people close to me.
4 In hours of crisis, I am more comfortable in depending on help extended by others rather than solely sticking with my own self-confidence, self-dependence or personal convictions.
5 I often get frightened with thoughts as if I am missing something significant in life and do feel a sense of emptiness at deeper level.
6 I know my own weaknesses well and hate myself for the same. That is why, on multiple occasions, I generally get impressed with traits of other people.
7 My work/profession absorbs me but only partially and I do wish I was actually engaged/employed in some other profession or occupation or company or location.
8 I seldom get to spend time in complete silence or solitude because there is no end to my 'To Do' list of pending jobs. My responsibilities tire me completely.
9 Best of efforts rarely succeed in getting me what I wish or deserve, as most of the time I end up getting rewarded lesser than my expectations.
10 I do get pangs of anxiety and sense of panic while worrying about things to come. I wish my future was more secure.
11 At times I do feel sense of frustration generating the urge to scream at the top of my voice.
12 I wish my life partner was more appreciative, considerate and accommodating and children more obedient and adhering to my suggestions.
13 If the burden of worldly responsibilities on my shoulders was lesser, I would have taken a different course of action to connect with my spiritual self.
14 My own self-interests or personal values are not strong enough as I am just not able to avoid or ignore impact of my decisions on my nears and dears.
15 I do blame my family circumstances during the growing years. If things were different, I would have pursued my passions and interests.

A total score of all above fifteen statements in excess of fifty points shows you operating under influence of your artificial self or fictional self. Total score falling between thirty to fifty suggest that you are disconnected with your authentic self and suffer from a level of uncertainty and skepticism about your own self. People falling in fifteen to thirty score range are well connected with their authentic self and are ideals for others around.

Some scholars also use another method to help you find out your own connection with your authentic self. Under this method, you are provided with a big basket of words representing a specific 'human quality' existing in different individuals. Such a list may have words representing both positive and negative traits. You are asked to make two copies of the list. Before going for the test, you are expected to do some thinking and identify few or handful heroes who happens to be your ideals in different life spheres. These may well be real people you genuinely appreciate, and wish to be like, or purely hypothetical image of your ideal. Similarly, such person(s) may be living or dead, older or younger, from your culture or otherwise etc. After zeroing down about your heroes, please pick up the first copy and circle out features that you appreciate your ideal individual(s) for. Depending on your own judgment, let the total number of features be in between ten to fifteen. As a second step, and certainly after some gap, you should pick up the second copy of the same list and circle same number of features that describe you yourself. Number of features common in your own list and the list of your ideal(s) suggest the level of operation of your authentic self. Needless to mention that higher the number of similarities stronger is the case for your life being governed by authentic self and the vice versa. Among others, features included in such a list may go like:

> *Nice looking, appealing, spiritual, wise, friendly, strongly opiniated, unwavering morality, uncompromised ethics, honest under all circumstances, hardworking, warm hearted, helpful to others, empathetic towards needy, affectionate, enthusiastic, egocentric, self-disciplined, belligerent, health conscious, self-motivated, great communicator, creative, democratic, trend setter, fast learning, adaptable, flexible, hospitable, optimist, persistent, selfish, gentle, thoughtful, innovative, intelligent, crafty, attentive, reliable, inspiring, confident, independent, affluent, popular, self-sufficient, conventional, arrogant, brave, peace loving, carefree, submissive, zealous, big hearted, strategist.*

At this stage of our discussions, it may be a good idea to look at both downsides and upsides of living a life embedded in authentic self. As we already know, living life of fictional self is quite dangerous state of being as it diverts or absorbs or robs your life energy. Such life remains dominated by forced way of thinking, feeling and acting. Such a life brings toxic results not only for the person possessed but equally for those around as well.

Downside of living a life of authentic self

- People might avoid, ignore or just dislike you altogether.
- You may be constantly judged by others completely giving a different color to your real intentions.
- You may be called with different names going right up to unbearable extremes.
- Reconnection with authentic self results is stoppage to ongoing inner dialogues. This invariably leads to a feeling of emptiness. Those familiar with this know how painful it can be.
- There remains a risk of losing control over many things which looked under perfect control so long as the fictional self was in command.
- You are bound to lose many friends and so-called well-wishers because all 'friends for benefits' stop showing interest in you once your authentic self starts directing your actions.
- Since you no more adhere to norms approved by society and cultural traditions, you can expect many criticisms from leaders of your erstwhile groups.
- You have to be ready to face many vulnerable situations as your previous avatar will keep applying pull forces to bring you back to your previous form.

Upside of living a life of authentic self

- You start living a life founded on present moment, a life where you remain true to yourself.
- You get opportunity to follow your desires and passions without worrying about disappointments of others.
- People get tested for their love for you for what you are and not how you appear or presented yourself to them.

- Living life of authentic self allows you to shred your sheet of lies as now you remain comfortable to display all your sides, including the good, bad and ugly, without any coverings.
- Now you can be really intimate in your relationships as you know that people still with you are real genuine people and are there because of your own worth and not net worth.
- You can expect to have unhindered flow of all human qualities like trust, confidence, love, hate, jealousy alike, releasing a sense of freedom from earlier frustrations.
- Having started the work of choice, your Job is no more just a job. Now you begin experiencing sense of purpose, fulfilment and completion.
- There remains no need to carry the fake mask of false identity. You don't have to remember how you behaved with whom. You are same with everyone around.
- Entire burden of feeling responsible for family, friends and colleagues and social groups gets removed from your shoulders.
- You can genuinely enjoy peace of congruence.
- You can celebrate your beliefs, thoughts, feelings, emotions and behaviors.
- The artificially enforced rule book governing your earlier life paves way for a concise and simple living.

In conclusion, it is clear that all above aspects touched various sides of our core but not in any significant manner. Each of these helped us to look at our real self but only from specific angles, leaving the real core much away from the gaze. But understanding self is like excavating archeological treasure buried deep down and completely forgotten remains of earlier periods. The only logical choice you have is to begin scrapping thin layers of overburden to protect the treasures from breakages. Even if you so desire, how can you expect to reach to the core that you can't even recognize? To best prepare for the excavation, you need to clear the site of all shrubs or previously existing structures. Understanding all above concepts and aspects was that very part of our journey. Depending on various things, the efforts required in clearing the site vary from case to case, so patience and commitment must be kept high at all times. That the treasure is waiting to be found is the surest thing in the process.

3

Awareness for Own Self

Myths Surrounding Self

On so many levels, most human beings are similar but on specifics like retina scan and fingerprints, there is no possibility of finding a match with anyone alive or dead. On an individual basis, each one of us can claim having unique personality, characteristics, interests, talents, gifts, and strengths. Human beings are interesting species in other ways too as they come in all extremes. You do come across some divine characters operating from short distance of some people belonging to completely animal nature. There are people doing their best for humanity and those doing their worst. There are some operating on conscious and rational basis and others who do just the opposite. These divisions of extremes are indeed thoroughly embedded in the rise of *Homo sapiens* and one can surely conclude that humanity is blessed with both higher and lower brains, and that people at large are torn between reason and irrational drives for sex, survival, and perhaps love and hate as well.

Human beings have always been expanding their knowledge in many areas around them and achieved spectacular accomplishments but are unable to know their own basic nature, the very source of their existence. You can blame it on the complexities of the subjects. For example, subjects like origin of universe or beginning of life on earth, are indeed so complex and difficult to comprehend that best of human minds, and at all times, kept trying but are yet to scratch out some significant aspects of these problems. No wonder, those subjects continue to remain mysteries waiting to be unraveled. But complexities of events in antiquity should not apply to knowing own true nature. Since we live with our own consciousness from our very first memory and we know about the same on moment by moment, it is perplexing to listen that knowing our own self also is wrapped with innumerable mysteries. But instances are there where reality remains different than what it should have been and knowledge about Self is one of those strong instances.

And this division has been around for the longest time. Christian search for life in heaven, Buddhist search for Nirvana or Vedic search for Moksha, are all search for solution to finish this duality among people. Vedic sages arrived at the knowledge of 'self' by diving deep into own awareness and made astonishing discoveries and proclaimed "Aham Brahmasmi", meaning 'I myself is the Universe'. But most basic question to explore is to understand if this duality is innate or it is manmade. Because any chances of going back to its original form, its primal state, the one which is absolute and whole without any division, can be attempted only when it is manmade.

Being Homo Sapiens certainly comes to rescue for this cause. To quote Yuval Noah Harari, the author of Sapiens - A Brief History of Humankind, "Most mammals emerge from the womb like glazed earthenware emerging from a kiln – any attempt at remoulding will only scratch or break them. Human emerge from the womb like molten glass from the furnace. They can be spun, stretched and shaped with a surprising degree of freedom. This is why today we can educate our children to become Christian or Buddhist, capitalist or socialist, warlike or peace-loving." We are indeed blessed with a large brain, wide choice of tools and techniques, learning abilities as well as complex social structures and all these are boons for going back to our original self.

In normal situations, humanity has been banking on either psychology, philosophy, religion or spirituality to seek answers for the unknown. But even science, in spite of all its progress or billions of Dollars spent on research and what not, is unable to solve mystery about Self of a human being. Off late however, unprecedented progress has been achieved in the field of neuroscience after making lots of efforts and finally we have some clues about the working of human mind. But much of that progress also is nothing more than scratching over the surface. Afterall, all sciences are based on investigable facts, analysis of data, and measurements of physical phenomena, which all are just not available for working of human mind. Using all the scientific progress achieved so far, the best we say is that self-awareness is very much a physical function of brain, capable of being monitored, accessed and analyzed.

On the other hand, we have testimonies of thousands of people over thousands of years who, through their own individual contemplations, meditative practices of self-inquiry, or some such techniques, could explore 'self' and produced results which can be called similar in nature. Summary of feedback from such people coming from diverse backgrounds cutting across time and cultural/geographical/religious dispensations, have remarkable similarities in terms of 'self' being ever present, silent, blissful, source of love, intelligent, creative, imaginative, full of insights, and not bound by time and space. Besides those selected few, almost all people who made worthwhile attempt on those tools and techniques and could achieve some degree of personal evolution, do confirm about foggy existence of non-duality. In short, it is almost agreed by all such seekers that the sense of 'self' is bottom line of every human existence.

On the other hand, some people call Self to be just a story, a constructed narrative created by one's brain. They argue that brain is the one which provide us identity of being what we are. They talk about compelling evidence coming from unfortunate individuals having partially damaged brain due to accident, disease or simply aging, the personality of such person gets changed so radically that the new version behaves in entirely different way than their previous versions. Similarly, some people alter their brain working artificially by use of drugs and are seen behaving and thinking differently. So, does the brain actually create illusion of our separate identity? Brain indeed does construct model of external as well as internal world and weaves experiences into a cohesive story. Mind also helps us to predict things likely to happen in future. But no brain is capable of producing non-physical experiences similar to what a Conscious Self is capable of doing almost constantly.

Yet another argument suggest that we are the 'Prana', the life breadth. But breathing is quite visibly a mechanical exercise involving inhaling and exhaling. We do feel it and can always tell if we are inhaling or exhaling. So, breathing also is just another activity of the body and its systems. Now, there is someone or something that is doing all this watching or feeling. This is the question before us, and the very purpose of this book is to have good clarity about who is doing all that watching and feeling, or "Who am I." That will mean knowing what is Enlightenment, what is Wisdom, what is Bliss, what is real Existence and finally what is being the 'Being'. That shall be known as the 'Truth'. Most importantly, we do not have to seek this truth outside as it is our own Self through which we can opt for searching for that truth.

Unfounded myths and misconceptions are known barriers in developing right understanding for any serious subject and 'Understanding Self' is no different. Some of these may be because of lack of sufficient clarity about concepts and philosophies involved and few others are because of wrong propaganda by people with destructive agendas.

Let us pick some of the popular myths in a random order.

1. Understanding Self is just a boring exercise—Because we live with our own self all our life, mind's very first reaction to the process of learning more in detail is always the obvious i.e., "I already know everything about self and this exercise is useless as there is nothing new to be learned." Mind is programmed to warn you against new learnings. Ego believes that everything is known and mind is lazy. Conclusion from these two factors combined is absolutely predictable. This initial reaction from our mind is natural to be expected for every new subject. But nothing can be far from truth.

Yes, a normal person lives with his self but there is always so much more to be learned and re-learned. New revelations about self are not only exciting in nature, they also bring a lot of ease in living life. Knowing new things about your own self is a very pleasing and enjoyable process, provided you are open for new learning and got the courage to see your own personal contents with naked eyes, without any bias or shades. The desire to learn must germinate from the desire to bring in improvement where ever required. Again, as normal human beings, we have to cross this bridge for every new learning, provided off course, if we wish to grow. Get ready to go over pains involved in learning new things to be a responsible being. Let us say that it is going to be the biggest self-improvement project one may have ever undertaken or thought about. How can that be anything other than exciting, exuberant and fulfilling?

2. It will dig out skeletons from past—The process of learning about self certainly involves bringing out all challenging aspects of your life including those you hate to recollect. Old bruises and skeletons are yours and remain with you no matter what. All unwanted and unliked past memories are extra dead weight you carry on shoulders. Even when you mentally avoid them and try pushing under the carpet, their burden always looms large. Psychologically, such incidents always keep working behind the scene and continue impacting your behaviors and responses indirectly. And why your process must begin with bad things only? You have the option to begin with all likeable aspects and keep less likable aspects for later, for the stage when you are more capable of dealing with adverse influence of even bad things from past. You will be better off to take areas which you did not know up until now followed by areas where you yourself knew that improvements are required. This itself covers more than half of your journey. Later, this issue will seize to exist of its own.

Pleasure and pains are both myths and you have no option but to cross them at some point to gain peace. Your situation at the time those incidences took place may have been hard, but you must have evolved from that position already. As you truly become familiar with your pleasure and pain triggering factors, your old experiences may also turn to give you more confidence and courage. Knowing your self with clarity, you get better to enjoy your experiences, where to find them, what they feel like, and how to avoid them. All this increases your baseline of happiness and resilience.

3. Knowing Self is a Selfish drive—Agreed that most adults have tons of responsibilities including towards spouse, children and work. Finding time required to invest in tools and techniques for exploring self might indeed sound selfish to some. But if you go to gym with the aim of improving your wellness, are you going to be blamed being selfish? Aren't you willing to do so many things to improve wellbeing of your loved ones? Is it selfish to work hard in your profession/occupation and achieve your full potential? It can never be selfish to improve yourself, even if the whole world screams for your attention and help.

If you are committed to put in hard work to stand for what is right, please remember that putting hard work required for mastering and taking good care of yourself is very much part of that very hard work. Actually, your wellbeing is a matter of celebration for your loved ones. Understanding self better goes to uplift quality of your interactions with each of them and that is certainly a positive development. In addition, you will be able to operate in your work or profession with added clarity. So, it is a win-win for all concerned. You are advised not to undertake this pious process for your own sake but please do not shy away from starting it for the sake of your loved ones. It will be great favor for them.

4. Understanding Self is about controlling mind—Many teachers and authors are seen advocating Self exploration to control the mind to perform on desired lines and get focused on desired objects/subjects. But such an approach is all farce and due for falling flat. People try hard for decades but fail to bring their mind under any degree of control because, by very nature, all efforts of controlling human mind are destined to fail. The DNA of human mind does not recognize 'no-fly-zones'. So, please guard against your desire to use this knowledge to control your mind in any significant manner.

Thoughts are the result of working of human mind. Similar to other organs like kidney, liver or heart, we have to let our mind work for what it is designed, thinking. All you do by understanding its working, is to channelize the same towards positive and productive outcomes. Mind has a predictable mechanism like other complex machines. Human mind hates vacuum even for a second. Mind and its processes are constantly working for indulging in desires or avoiding aversions. This indulgence and avoidance are like two monkeys living on a single tree, our mind; while they continue to shake and agitate the tree, it is futile to expect total peace or total control. However, what is left unsaid is that better results require training those monkeys in desired manner. Once they get suitably trained, they will jump but in right direction.

What best can be done to regulate the mind, however, will be taken up in much greater details in due course.

5. Knowing Self is best done under Guidance of seasoned Teachers or Experts—This is a total misconception that Understanding Self is dependent on others. This view gets formed due to complex nature of the subjects involved in the process. Learning about self is tougher than one thinks; it demands lots of discipline and dedication, but it is more of an art than science and hence, need to be learned by developing conceptual understanding and self-practice alone. Others have but only a limited role out here and that too only in initial phase.

Talking on a subtle level, each one of us is blessed with different orientations and no outsider can ever know or track what goes in our mind 24/7. Knowing self is like learning underwater swimming in a large tunnel on a dark night. No one is around at the moment when it matters. Each person must dig his own well to quench his thirst. No one ever finds heaven with the dying of others. If heaven is what you need, please be ready to go through death yourself.

Exploring inner core is not knowledge which can be acquired or taught. Our own truth must be accessed by us singularly with our own efforts. Experiences of others are good to get general directions. But in tough topography you need to make your own way. The path is accidented with serpentine trails and passes through the bushes filled with lots of uncertainties. You alone have the power of making your way through it. You must be ready to fall or get lost. Prepare yourself to retract, rearrange, re-motivate and keep going. Holding somebody's hand may save you from some falls or some detours but will rob your chances to pursue your own individual unique destination.

6. Knowing Self is escape from something or someone—No, it is not about avoiding harsh realities or escape into emptiness. Knowing self stops you from running away from real understanding of your core in its true form. It is about finding right answers to all questions one may have and removal of all doubts paving way for pure wisdom. It is a process to help you get over your psychological pains. You will get your mood swings even after knowing your core better. Knowing your self does not quash or terminate your feelings and inadequacies. Even after knowing your core, you continue remaining open for ups and downs offered by human life.

But a person operating with authentic self gains ability to use better tools to deal with normal tenacious realities of actual human life. It enhances your acceptance for those realities. You need not push them under the carpet as you gain courage to deal with them fair and square. In due course, your knowledge about self also heightens your observation skills as well as your awareness. Those traits help you in facing fears and scars and getting over them with objectivity and practical approach. This process makes your dark shadows stand in front of you forcing to see through all grey shades of your personality. So, there is no escaping from any issue or person.

7. Knowing Self risks profound/transcendental experience—Experiencing is nothing but an art of accumulating greed for repeating the same feeling later. Further, all experiences are always grounded in past. Increased awareness about self on the other hand, focuses on present with complete delinked connection with past or future. And, focus on present does not involve any accumulations as it runs in real time.

Self-exploration involves reaching to deeper levels of sub consciousness and that is neither an experience nor a matter of qualitative ecstasy. All you try doing is to reach to your own originality, purity, and natural spontaneity. Transcendental experiences are just imaginary myths and hold no place in real life.

In the process of exploring our realm, we practice silence which succeed in temporarily taming the mental process to relative tranquility. That also slows down the agitation in the mind forcing a sharp drop in overall energy levels. Such drop induces dullness moving from subtle to gross and finally leading to strong drowsiness. Unfortunately, some naïve beginners take such experiences too seriously and, purely out of their ignorance, call them profound. You can just laugh out such observation as figment of imagination.

In reality, transcendental experience presupposes a non-dual state of awareness where one gets perception of a subtle pure being. Such being is without any phenomenon, distraction, intention, desire or even thinking. It is a state where default mode of the being switches from ego to consciousness, where there is no world of senses, objects or thoughts. In this state there is no doer, no process, no action and no thinker. Well, such a state is technically possible but only for someone who has reached the pinnacle of progress in his practice. Fearing it at the initial stage of journey is too much to imagine.

8. Knowing Self involves unraveling of mysteries—A common thread among all different definitions of mystery is 'something not understood or beyond understanding'. While our subject deals with going deeper to consciousness, something deeper than thoughts, but there is nothing mysterious about it. Yes, a person just starting this journey may suffer for a while from the fear of unknown. This process involves intricate use of mind to know about itself and later overcome the deficiencies noticed by the same mind. It is like a single person acting as investigator and judge for a cold-blooded murder trial. The only way to demystify this enigma is through constant practice and experience.

In the end, process of knowing own core holds power to change all types of perspectives, attitudes and mental processes. Prolonged efforts alone begin to unravel all mysteries buried down in an ignorant mind, one at a time. We may expect fine tuning of our sensory system allowing us to listen to our own conscience or Antahkarana, with clarity but that is about all. Knowing self also is a skill and must be practiced as such. It is similar to most other skills and is to be acquired, practiced and mastered rather than something genetic or God's gift. What gets revealed is not something exceptional but the real truth that was always there in the depth of our being, the one that remained invisible, suppressed or overburdened under ignorance or false understanding.

Knowing self reconnects us to our own core by cutting through layers of burden laid by ego dominated attitudes and habits. Once we reach there with our own efforts, bit by bit, one baby step at a time, we realize beautiful eternal reality of being human. For sure, there is no place for mysteries here.

9. Self-knowledge relaxes you and calms you down from stressful situations— Knowing yourself is neither a way of getting a sense of serenity or rejuvenation in any way. But it is not to say that it does not lead to relaxed or calmness in general. As we shall see, the process involves practicing many tools and techniques like Yoga, Pranayam, Meditation and many more. One is bound to experience slowing heart rate, lowering blood pressures, relaxation of muscles and increased blood flow to mind.

But let us remember that such physical benefits are purely incremental in character and incidental in nature. You get them on the way rather than you working exclusively to get them. Knowing self involves internal reflections, introspections and ultimately achieving deeper states of consciousness. Physical benefits out of this process, at best, is similar to starters being served before the main course. So, please do not eat too much of starters as it ends up reducing your appetite by the time main course, the real nourishment, get served.

10. Understanding Self is a self-improvement project—All big improvements demand changes in attitudes and behaviors. Actually, the very thought of self-improvements emanates from an unending sense of lacking something substantial, a sense of unworthiness. This tricky feeling gets formed with ongoing self-blames and poor sense of self-judgement by the critic sitting within. Without going in nitty-gritty of these issues the very desire of self-improvement is a faulty concept as it starts from the belief that something is less than ideal. As against this, we got concept of acceptance, the virtue of being happy and satisfied with things as they exist. These two concepts stand in diametrically opposite corners of contradictions.

With reference to matured adults, the very inclination towards self-improvement works as a trap. Longing for improvement arises from wanting more of what you already got. Striving more calls for ongoing evaluation and judgement on progress being achieved where forming wrong judgement continuously becomes a way of life. This cycle got no end to it. In the least, this cycle keeps mind engaged on issues away from 'here and now'. A mind that is eternally busy in attempting for a better circumstance is certainly busy even after achieving set targets and, in the process, bound to generate dissatisfaction and sufferings. Just imagine the additional impacts of failures and frustrations due to under achieving of targets?

In contrast to all this, knowing self asks you to live in the present moment, the only true moment of life. A person involved in self-criticism is inflicting severe kind of violence upon himself. Practices suggested to shine Self strive for self-compassion and self-acceptance which necessarily leads to contentment. A person already blessed with contentment has different meaning of self-improvements as his focus shifts to self-realization instead. Let us say at this moment that working on self-actualization and self-realization are far greater objectives than self-improvements and our process of understanding self does focusses on those very supreme objectives.

11. Such practices are only for Saints—For long time, exploring Self has been associated with people living in caves or mountains, the saints and sages from across cultures or hermits/ascetics belonging to ancient Indian traditions. All these people are highly revered in their respective faith systems. These people are known to survive under climatically challenged circumstances which are beyond the threshold limits applicable for commoners. But reality about exploring Self is a different story altogether as there is nothing that limits exploration of self only for selected few. This exploration can be undertaken by every living person who is able to feel and think or, using intellectually sounding interpretations, who is able to reflect, ponder and contemplate.

Age, gender, education, occupation, social or psychological background, or religious orientation, make no difference for moving on with knowing yourself. However, people having positive orientation towards devotion, religion and philosophy are seen better placed for making faster progress on this path for obvious similarities in the process involved. Knowing one's own deeper spectrum in true light is equally helpful for scientists, artists, eccentrics or tricksters. It has been helpful to people from ancient times but its relevance in today's fast paced, stress generating, competitive and materialistic life has increased significantly; it is an age-old tool having proven efficacy and equally effective for new ailments. It is very much for Karma Yogis of the real world like us. The only condition is that it requires strong willpower for getting transformed into a newer, purer, yourself.

12. Understanding Self is a religious practice—This practice may have been followed by people from a certain background in the past. But it has always largely been a practice for achieving spiritual goals. And spirituality has always begun above the place where religion or all other man-made divisions seize to exist. In its present context, it does not get associated exclusively with any religion or culture in particular. Anyone and everyone can undertake this exercise and get benefited without even basic belief in anything divine. An Atheist or an Agnostic may practice and seek benefit as much as a Christian or Muslim or Hindu or Buddhist, as it does not come in any conflict with any faith at all. It will make you a better version of your own self irrespective of whatever you may have been. And after gaining certain level of success in this drive, you will not even have the desire to restrict yourself with any limited sphere like a particular religion as you begin to see the entire humanity in an unique interconnected way.

13. It takes years to get any benefit—The answer is a big no because benefits of knowing yourself start accruing immediately and keep growing with the progress of your efforts. It is like learning to play a sport. Even on the very first day on it, you stand to gain the physical advantages to the least. The low hanging fruits like calming of mind, lowering of mental tensions, prioritizing your time and energy as well as identifying important things to attend to, do not take much long to begin flowing.

Superior level benefits, however, may take varying periods and efforts depending on so many other factors. All other things remaining same, length of practice and cumulative benefits can be considered growing in similar directions. Understanding self has many levels of benefits. However, benefits like better mental health, a bit more peace and balance in your life, start trickling in few months itself. You will usually feel better after every single concerted effort you make to know yourself better.

14. We may have to abandon life and become a monk—As a cricket lover, you are ill advised to stop playing your game fearing that you might become a Dhoni or Kohli. Becoming a better version, a complete version, a genuinely original version of your own self can never generate a fear of abandoning normal life. It is too distant a fear to worry as there are far more important immediate hurdles to cross. But off course, if you are indeed deeply spiritual type who feels trapped in worldly attractions and living worldly life under pressures from family or culture, you might gain desired confidence to give up the world of senses and walk out to live a different life. And thinking loudly, if one is really having natural orientation of living an ascetic life, should he not walk out of the normal life for beginning to live life as a monk? But at this stage, it is too far-fetched a danger.

15. Technology/Medical interventions can be used to perfect our Self—In today's time and world, it is natural to look towards technologies to provide easy solution to our daily life problems. Even in the brain functioning field, there are scanning technologies detecting working of our mind at a given point of time. Such feedback can be very useful for exact analysis which were not possible just a couple of years earlier. But knowing yourself is not about just knowing the things; it is all about comprehension and realization. Besides knowing, bringing desired changes involves too many right efforts and there is no possibility of inventing a magic pill that can direct us to our inside by directly cutting through all those normal things going through in our body systems.

Some people take various kind of drugs to experience altered states of consciousness but that is closer to intoxication. No, unfortunately, technology has not found any solution to cut down on efforts required to know your deeper core. For thousands of years the ancient people all over the world have been experimenting newer and newer methods for redemption from illusions or expanding consciousness but to no avail. True awakening, the main purpose of this effort, does not get served in any way by support from technology or any other support from outside.

Fact remains that technology and sciences have only been successful in scratching outer surface of working of a human mind. There are still no instruments to help understand working of its subtle systems. Practices recommended to establish better connect with your core, mostly hover around knowledge, awareness, serenity, one-pointedness, self-control, and technologies, sciences and other medical interventions do not contribute as such on those fronts, at least as things stand today. But tomorrow may be a different world, who knows.

16. Knowing Self makes you emotionless—Emotions play important role in most aspects of intrapersonal, interpersonal as well as social and cultural levels. There is no doubt that emotions have crucial role on our psychological composition and bring a lot of meaning for living life as an individual, or in relationships with all others groups and societies. Life will be dull without the treasure of our feelings or joy from sports and arts. Besides pleasure of physical contacts with the loved ones and fun with friends, even negative emotions like sadness, anger or fear go in making life a lot more meaningful. Emotions work like any rapid information system and initiate action without involving much thinking. Humanity owes its survival to fast actions initiated under influence of emotions all over our evolutionary process. Without emotions we may not have been able to make faster decisions in tight situations like when to attack or defend, to flee or hide, to enjoy particular food or reject, to love a person or hate, etc. Emotions differentiate us from machines and inspire us to learn, work hard and belong. Loss of emotions is a big sacrifice to ask from any human being.

But, rather than making you emotionless, the whole process of understanding self significantly sharpens your perceptions of all sense organs and helps you feel more deeply and clearly. It lets us feel real hints coming to surface, both from within, without or from others being interacted with, that otherwise would have remained ignored. It simply enables us to operate from a deeper place inside ourselves, a place that is larger than our emotions and concerns.

17. Knowing Self is just being narcissistic—Many ignorant people do carry this impression that it is just another fashionable tag that modern hypocrites discuss about in drawing room talks to impress each other and, to that extent, it is just another thing like materialistic possessions or positions used to put one on a podium higher than others, a showoff exercise. This is a harmless but very dangerous misconception. Self exploration exercise generally shows painful things previously unknown. It introduces us to our true nature and real response drivers of our actions and reactions and, at times, we never knew that darker side of ourselves. This process is certainly going to repeatedly show us that we are just an average human being with all normal frailties. Some people do resort to nasty behaviors, under influence of such feeling, but there is no known risk for that for bulk of the majority.

Knowing self is all about knowing reality as it exists without any ifs and buts, without any pre-existing image or false desire, without getting conditioned to what is socially correct or incorrect. In most cases, real knowledge of self is inversely reverse of 'feel good' factor. As your observation gets sharper, your mind gets quieter, and you start looking clearer, you may comfortably see even parts of yourself that are not pretty. Knowing your core is a very serious skill to acquire and people who wish to indulge into 'feel good' factors are in for a rude shock. No, knowing your self is not for people going after glitter but only for those gold diggers who do not mind removing tons of over burden in search of potential gold hidden somewhere down below.

18. Self-exploration is 'The only thing' to do—Propagating this exploration as an ultimate solution for all problems in areas such as health, wellness, growth, or enlightenment will be exaggeration. You may call it a must undertake mission, one that is highly essential but not the only activity required for a complete and successful human life. It is expected to dissipate some of your negative mental patterns, manage your emotions better, help you have better control over your thoughts, let you see yourself as an entity beyond your body/mind and provide insight into the nature of your Self but there are many other aspects of life that still need to be addressed separately.

For example, you will still need to have good financial planning to meet your bills, you need to remain connected with ever evolving technologies to interact and respond socially, you need to increase your knowledge and wisdom about subjective world and its working, and beyond all of this, you need to make use of insight developed knowing yourself better to make changes in your life, and in life of people in immediate circle of influence.

Better knowledge about self might also help you to have better relationships, but you still need to do self-reflection and tweak your undesirable behaviors. It will help you grow as a human being, but you will still be challenged, day after day, with the need of making the right choices. It will give you a peak into enlightenment, but you will still need to be cautious such that ego does not bounce back soon after somebody stepping on your foot. That is the precise reason that self-exploration is called a practice, a journey with no destination.

Ego and its Working

Ego is our conscious identity that an untrained normal mind equates with his 'self'. Ego experiences the sense of everything associated with 'me' 'mine' and 'I'. It touches every aspect of our worldly existence and work as a catalyst for enjoying experiences, perceptions, memories, knowledge and relationships. Ego remembers, evaluates, plans, and in other ways is responsive to and acts in the surrounding physical and social world. Ego manages almost everything between 'me' and world at large. Life without ego would just turn out to be dull and dumb. It is our all-weather best friend, and best advocate defending 'me' at all times and with all its might. Ego makes you stand apart from every other person and thrives in uniqueness and prompts you to do things differently to leave lasting impressions on all others. It has indeed helped humanity immensely in advancing all over its evolutionary process. To that extent it is not a bad word in any way.

When does it forms? Initially when a baby is born, it is unable to distinguish between the internal and the external world. It is not able to differentiate its image from an object's image. Apart from this, a child can only perceive his body as partial objects, not as a whole. Over time, and due to the first interactions with the child's mother, the Ego begins to emerge. Sometimes between six and eighteen months of age, a child starts recognizing himself as an 'I'. Later its superior version starts maturing by involving inhibitions of instincts and control of impulses. At this stage itself, ego starts absorbing all parental and social norms the child gets exposed to. Soon his own unique standards start taking shape telling him what is right and what is not. At this stage the picture turns murkier as multiplicity of this process infuses host of confusions and conflicts bringing competing conclusions. This process gives rise to different defense mechanisms. And this process continues on and on, all over our physical life.

Ego is a unity of body, mind, life and intelligence. It is not a mere flux but a conscious awareness which becomes live only when intelligence works as a unifying force within other three elements. Human memory is the dominant factor that facilitate continuity of Ego besides many other factors operating largely on subconscious level. An individual ego remains covered by ignorance when it believes itself to be different from all other egos. This sense of separation itself is called 'Ahamkara' which is blamed for preventing harmony and unity of the person with the Universe at large. Physical sufferings and mental agonies are said to be due to failure of this very lack of harmony. The moment the veil of ignorance is taken away by gaining required wisdom, prevailing ignorance paves way for the person to move up from all selfishness in his system, gaining his happiness and unity with everything in surroundings. For many people Ego is equal to self, which is not the case in reality.

Ego is our best advocate and like every other advocate, it fights the case of its only client without any concern of the real truth. It continues justifying its client's stand even when he is brazenly wrong. Incidentally, ego is a fiction created in the mind and by the very mind. In all simplicity, our ego is an illusionary image founded on narrow views and interests. That is why ego bonds well with the mind and their joint working results in popping up most intelligent logic and rationale behind even stupid responses of the owner.

Materialist Perspective of Ego

In its materialist perspective, ego is identified on a physical or material level. The materialist perspective is simply a person's sense of self-significance, the very part of mind that mediates between the conscious and unconscious. In this role it is responsible for letting us test reality and feel the sense of separate identity. Originating from Latin with literal meaning 'I', ego is the name card, a mark of identity and individuality, we use while introducing our self to the rest of the world. Each one of us spend a great deal of our time and attention in establishing this ego, exalting it, defending it, championing it and conserving it. It also provides us super inflating feeling of pride. Since our ego defines and perpetuates our self-concept, self-construct, self-identity as well as self-perspective, it is quite unlikely for someone to have any aversion against it. Ego puts you in the center of the entire Universe and doesn't hesitate to project you as supreme expression of creation.

Ego remains super busy in making comparisons of every big and small interaction and such comparisons get interplayed with the binary of likes and dislikes. Ego constantly classifies all actions, thoughts, words, opinions, views and practically entire mental content, both our own as well as of others in touch with us, and qualitatively judges them as good, bearable, agreeable or otherwise. In this process, Ego imprisons poor mind and manipulates it to take wrong judgements under the colors of our unique separate existence. Detailed understanding of this point goes to help us appreciate our behavior under different situations.

> *"The ego is only an illusion, but a very influential one. Letting the ego-illusion become your identity can prevent you from knowing your true self. Ego, the false idea of believing that you are what you have or what you do, is a backwards way of assessing and living life."* — Wayne Dyer

Ego's ability to judge and giving precedence to self-esteem, together with its ability to wrongly influence mind's working, are main reasons as to why it requires a detailed and critical look. Like an elephant walking through the market, Ego looks at everything and calls every stuff in categories like 'like it', 'do not like it', 'pick it', 'chose it', 'appreciate it', 'ignore it' or even 'hate it'. This single aspect of ego fuels the span of working of all human emotions and feelings. Ego makes us irrationally selective and forces us to take a stand on everything either 'for' or 'against'. This discrimination fuels the labelling of strong likes and dislikes. Initially, these likes and dislikes may sound rather harmless but on cumulative basis, they snowball into extreme positions similar to differentiating hell from heaven. That is why this struggle is rightly labelled as worst disease of human mind because it impedes search for truth. Ego is best.

Desires, cravings, attention, arrogance, attachments, pride and envy are Ego's common tricks that get used very frequently. Layered memories of these tricks create a blinding effect as the shades of our lenses get subjectively colored. That is how normal people lose the purity of their vision and begin seeing things from their own biased angle. Since ego puts too much emphasis on 'me', it ends up creating distance with most others. Its craving for 'me' being unique, it keeps creating false projections always pitching you against others. As an extension of this, ego creates unrealistic, self-obsessed and self-admiring false moral idealism. Allowing it to continue indulging on advancing our self-esteem ultimately turns into one of the biggest evil prevailing in humanity.

The wise people say that perfect way is impossible for those who 'pick and choose' and that everything starts appearing clear the moment influence of ego is crossed over. Unfortunately, ego tells us that what we know is sufficient and there is no need to know more or learn afresh. Thus, ego proves the biggest roadblock in our journey of self-discovery. That is why knowing the working of Ego is enlightening. Ego centric mentality has to be crossed over at all costs. Once Ego's game plan stands exposed in clear light, doors to so many alternative options begin to open of its own on the basis of right understanding and new learnings, correct interpretation and new knowledge about self and others alike.

> *"Ego is just like dust in the eyes. Without clearing the dust you can't see anything clearly. So, clear the ego and see the world." (www.wisdomquotesandstories.com)*

Spotting Ego in Action

Before going ahead with spotting ego at work and making any worthwhile measurement of the same, let us divide quality of ego in two extremes and label them as 'normal' and 'authentic' ego respectively. The difference between these extremes can be observed by alternate responses to a given situation, as per examples below. The limited purpose of this categorization is to help the reader see the potential difference in how things 'are' and how they could have been:

- How can I impress others with my abilities vs what can I create, to remain engaged with something interesting?
- How can I protect myself and receive as much love and respect as one can have in this world vs how much can I contribute using my creativity and ability to make this world a happier place where people get desired love and respect?
- How to ensure that people come to me and seek my favor/blessings vs how can I connect with others and learn from their traits and experiences?
- How can others help me living a luxurious life vs what all can I cultivate, build, and grow for others to enjoy and experience?

Ego may be visible in most mundane acts. The symptoms indicating quality of ego of a person under evaluation are very obvious and hard to ignore. All you need is a keen and dispassionate observation for things happening in your surroundings. Having clarity about insights, displaying capacity to make long term plans, ability to incorporate results of alternate course of events, ability to apply plain logic and reasoning in making choices, high level of resistance against temptations, ability to skirt around social pressures or standard norms, are all clear indicators of 'authentic' quality of the ego of the doer under scan. On the other hand, a person displaying signs such as impulsive behavior, inferiority complex, fragility, low level of emotional stability, high level of vulnerability, bigger gaps between reality and perceptions, high level of insecurities, self-doubts and greater need for external validation, may any time be taken as a person operating under 'normal' ego syndrome.

Let us now quickly settle curiosity for identifying ego at work within our internal systems. All you need to do is pick up a question, think hard, recollect real life recent examples of the scenario and count how many affirmative replies are collected. Besides getting 'yes' for an answer, the strength of yes ranging from 'for sure Yes' to a simple 'may be' or 'more likely' may be used to measure vertical variations. Conducted over different periods, the count and their vertical intensity will provide you a clear direction of the progress made as well. Since these examples are picked up from normal life, readers may not have much problem in establishing direct connection with these questions:

1. Do you look forward to appreciation from others? Do you feel flattered when people praise your thoughts, mannerism or behaviors?
2. How much pressure you feel for your criticism by others? Do you react and try to put things in order as and when you hear people criticizing you? How long you remain upset and lose mental peace over such criticism?
3. Do you feel offended when another person gets credit for your efforts and initiatives? Do you feel the urge of letting others know that you deserve the credit more than others?
4. Are you generally ok when your friends or family members deal with their own issues without seeking your opinion, suggestions or approval? Do you get worked up when they do not work as per your advice? Do you really believe yourself to be wiser than them on matters relating to living life properly?
5. How eager you get to justify your position and putting things in right perspective every time others find fault with your views? What is your sensitivity level and to what extent will you go to prove your point?
6. Do you seek attention of people of your inner circle on your opinions, skills, actions and achievements? How often you try to project your behavior as ideal or exemplary?
7. Do you seek approval of others for your lifestyle? do you secretly desire to be taken as a role model by people at home, work and in your social networks?
8. Are you ready to jump in with your inputs even before other people finish putting their views? What is your level of excitation to do so?
9. Do you indulge in mental judgments over actions and words of others? How often you wish others had acted or responded in ways you deem fit?
10. How often you feel satisfied with inputs and suggestions provided by other members in your teams? How often you find others falling short of your expectations?

Should We Resist/Protest against our Ego

Ego works like a soccer coach on the sidelines who is always engaged seeing the big picture and swap out players, determine strategy, keep everyone motivated, steer the whole organization, and provides meaning and purpose, without being on the field. Ego's overbearing presence is really that much which is surely too much. At times, one does get tired of it and wishes to get rid of it. But that is just not an option on the table. All one can do is try loosening its grip. But such desire demands very strong efforts. Ego knows well that giving up its hold is nothing short of death, and like every other living being, ego is also afraid to die.

The moment Ego feels under attack, it panics and comes out defending ever so strongly. While under attack, it makes use of every dirty trick at its command. It already knows well how to befool the mind itself, so using deception, it submits before the owner and promises to behave ever so correctly. But as soon as it gets opportunity to bring its hold back, it returns to its original form in rather quick times. However, it can be purified to desired level using a long-drawn process demanding big efforts.

> *"The first half of life is devoted to forming a healthy ego, the second half is going inward and letting go of it."* — Carl Jung

Such purification is also called maturing of Ego, or evolving into authentic ego. An authentic ego, as noted through examples, sufficiently advances in growth to consider possibilities beyond 'me'. A matured ego begins to seek truth as it exists, without feeling fear or competition. Maturing ego by someone living on this earth is considered a beautiful and powerful gift for humanity. What we need is to attempt liberating our sense of self from this tiny little swamp called ego. Let us get convinced that we are not what our ego yells us we are; that we are not alone, that we got no reason to fight the truth, that we can never justify blame, hatred, or anger when we know the truth, and finally that we are free.

This process completes when one gets access to his deeper core and activate power of wisdom. Then alone, his sense of SELF moves up, bit by bit, in an incremental transformation. At that stage, mind can see through the illusions propagated by the ego. The person begins to understand the truth beyond seeming duality and comprehend what true freedom is. He turns his focus inward, his mind gains quietness and begins to explore its real contents. One may use any single or multiple techniques available for this purpose like yoga, pranayama, or meditation (all these techniques are rolled out in sufficient details in subsequent chapters). Once a person begins to learn focusing his mind, in a natural process, the incremental process of reclaiming of SELF can be said to begin.

That process requires total surrender with bend knees and folded hands. It demands your voluntary acceptance, with all humility, that you are just an ignorant being who is willing to forget everything from past and is ready for a new beginning. This is the process of spiritual advancement. This requires total liberation by abandoning all your thoughts, imaginations, beliefs, opinions, impressions and finally arriving at conclusion that as a humble being you cannot figure out anything and everything about your role in this universe; that leveled sense of emptiness or nothingness is the real indicator of evaporation of all ill effects of ego. In practical terms aiming for being egoless simply means putting others ahead of 'me' in every respect. Yes, this involves total transformation of self, one that is possible only by spiritual evolution. Egolessness is a state where you learn to exist simply as a witness to things happening around, where you do not get attached or identified even with your own thoughts.

Spiritual Perspective of Ego

This version of ego is also created by the false self as a product of conditioned mind. But in its spiritual perspective, ego is identified with individual's true self. Here also ego stands in between one's focus on here and now being on one side and state of pure attention on the other. It is called pure attention when there are no recurring thoughts, commentaries and evaluations. Normal spiritual ego also is limiting in nature and prevents us from expanding to infinite. But in its improved version, spiritual ego achieve transcendence to gain altered state of consciousness; one that is not bothered for any concern for self. At this stage, improved spiritual ego makes way for letting reality be perceived with greater objectivity.

The idea behind discussing Ego so much in detail is to ensure that Ego is unable to work as giant size speed breakers capable enough to derail all further efforts involved in developing true understanding about self. In order to ensure right progress, one must continue guarding against working of Ego until it broadens enough and emerges as transcendence of true self. Interestingly, this process requires you to first realize a strong and healthy ego with accentuated subjectivities before you make efforts to cross over that very subjectivity. You must become somebody before becoming nobody. In other words, you should become human before you become spiritual being. Just as a side reference, Western philosophy encourages the first part of this very sense of strong ego while Eastern philosophy advocates the second part.

Magnifying Awareness for Own Self

> *"Knowing others is intelligence; knowing yourself is true wisdom. Mastering others is strength; mastering yourself is true power."* — Lao Tzu

Being self-aware is by far the first step to correctly know your real self. It is only natural to feel that we have already been aware about everything. Enhanced self-awareness is an established key for initiatives intended towards bringing transformations in one's life. Actions of a self-aware person are always better aligned with his personal standards. This alignment helps in evaporating stress from this person's life and allows the freedom to live in present. That is why the complete process of becoming self-aware needs to be dealt with in sufficient details.

This process begins with the journey of self-discovery which is defined by American English dictionary 'as becoming aware of one's true potential, character, motives, etc.' A person interested in travelling through this tedious path is required to confront, and combat own fears and confusions. Discovery of self is truly comparable to an expert explorer studying the mountain to be climbed. He must explore it fully from all directions including its base, slopes, peaks and valleys. Self-awareness is our own Mount Everest that we aim to climb and conquer. A novice climber is well advised to prepare hard before initiating his climb else perishing into unknown ditches is always a real threat. Interestingly, this climbing expedition revels many wow moments on the way to the peak making the journey highly exciting and rewarding.

As we have seen, to begin with, self can be classified as Physical and Spiritual. Physical self consists of five elements coming together to make the physical body. Later mind, intelligence and ego get added to it. Together, all these eight make a unique 'me'. This 'me' is very obvious and visible and it operates with plethora of other sub-systems like emotions, likes-dislikes, feelings, attitudes, aptitudes, thoughts, desires, perceptions, memories etc. 'Me' is the main motive behind everything in life and quality of this very 'me' determines who we are at the end of the day. To begin with, this 'me' is just like a fresh canvas. Every interaction and experience of real life leaves its colored imprints on that canvas in subtle manner. Slowly, all through the growing period, the entire canvas gets colored where further brush strokes continue shading over the existing colors, layer by layer. This evolutionary process continues unabated in several directions, gradually growing more and more complex where demands and desires keep moving over from basics to superficial levels without any end in sight.

This part of self also includes a person's essential being, his core; specially considered as the object of introspection or reflexive actions. This part of the self is beyond ego syndrome and starts from the place where ego ends. Over the years of a person's life, all his traits, goals, aspirations, experiences, interests and every such other quality that go to differentiate him from others keep evolving and cementing this 'me' in more and more individualistic form. Also, this 'me' keeps enjoying that separateness and keep fueling it more and more.

Our 'me' guides us to discriminate rights from wrongs, activates our discretion and helps in formulating personal and social behavior. Imagine there was no dissuasion by internal discretion cautioning us against indulging in sense pleasures. Most of us would have certainly been worse off. The problem starts when, in ignorance, one starts pampering his 'me' too much. Pampered 'me' starts behaving in dictatorial manner with self-centered arrogance and starts actually believing that his 'me' is indeed superior. So much so that it starts expecting and, if possible, demanding respect from others. Later, he wishes to be feared and worshipped by one and all. Such individual starts feeling insulted with tiniest pricking.

> *"Finding yourself" is not really how it works. You aren't a ten-dollar bill in last winter's coat pocket. You are also not lost. Your true self is right there, buried under cultural conditioning, other people's opinions, and inaccurate conclusions you drew as a kid that became your beliefs about who you are. "Finding yourself" is actually returning to yourself. An unlearning, an excavation, a remembering who you were before the world got its hands on you.* — Emily McDowell

Self-awareness, once enhanced to desired levels, helps in improving understanding why we feel, act, think or behave the way we do. That is how it protects against ills arising from too much focus on our 'me'. Once we begin to be more self-aware, we get the opportunity to differentiate real right from wrong and finally obtain freedom to change things about our self, wherever required. This process alone enables us to live a life where our feelings, thoughts, actions and reactions get aligned to our own true reality. It is almost impossible to change and become self-accepting if we are not well aware about our self to begin with.

Well-developed self awareness is quite empowering and satisfying. Clarity obtained from being aware provides us confidence to initiate changes and convert them into reality. This eventually leads to improved generation of thoughts, which in turn, increases creativity and spontaneity. It sharpens the sensing capability of our sense organs. Improved awareness also fuels the desire to get high, a desire to get a kick required by most high performing individuals to obtain extraordinary results out of their efforts. The importance of self-awareness is like pathological tests for the internist to identify proper diagnostic conditions before prescribing right medications. Improving self-awareness succeeds only when administered like a long-drawn therapy.

Ways to Sharpen Self-Awareness

Simple statement as 'my hand' is enough proof that 'me' and my hand are two separate entities. One of these is an observer and the other subject of that observation. Let us call the first as 'The Observing self' and the second one as the 'material' or 'Physical Self'. For brevity, let us call the first one as the 'Seer'. On functional level, the 'seer' keeps witnessing everything happening at the other level. As and when an individual detaches his 'seer', from body, mind and the ego, the perception for everything around becomes clearer and deeper. Such a person perceives underlying motives for actions. He can spot his true intentions without any prejudice. This ability to separate the 'seer' from the subjective duality (me) is the art that get perfected with lots of efforts, off course. Such a person is aptly called Enlightened or with some such similar names. And it is not an impossible task as so many people, right here, among us, are able to achieve this distinction. The need is to look at this with a practical approach rather than an intellectual exploration. Let us get out of the notion that only exceptional people can realize their duality of their self. No, it can be achieved by any normal person with efforts and practice. Such understanding is essential before undertaking available ways and means to achieve transformations.

Difficulties in Becoming Self-Aware

The reference to self is always open-ended to include ongoing experiences, at present, this very moment, before it turns over to past. For a non-attentive person, this moment gets passed by even before its realization sets in. That is why generally most of us remain busy either in past or worrying for things to come. But both past and future are unwanted roadblocks in becoming self-aware. Right realization of pointlessness of past and futility of future has immense power of freeing us from chains of undesired prison. The smell of fresh flowers can be enjoyed only when we decide to live in present.

On this note, becoming self-aware should be a cake walk because we know ourselves so well and nobody else is involved in the process. But the reality is just the

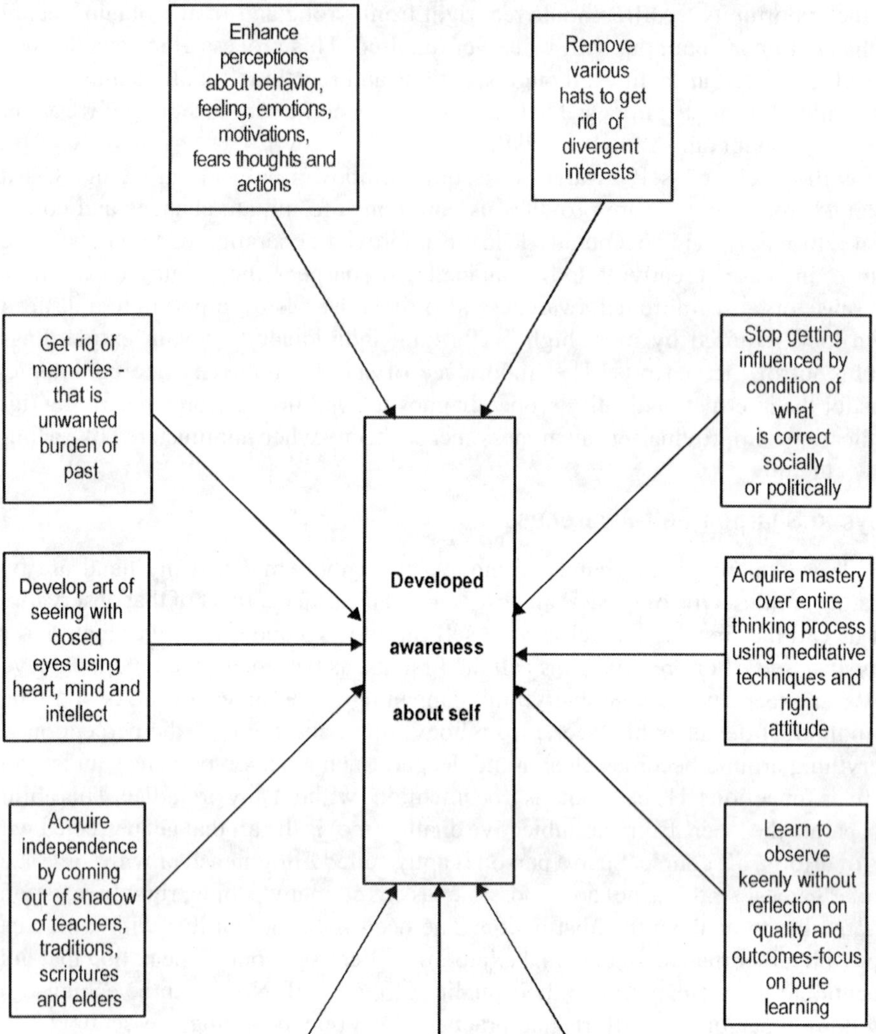

Fig.: Managing Self-Awareness

opposite. To bring about the transformation required right down to our attitude level, whole lot of reverse process for de-layering of strokes is required. Interestingly, the only instrument available to work is mind alone. As seen earlier, in normal state, this very mind is seen as captured by ego with all its allurements and false trappings. This is where the complexities arise as same mind is to divide itself into different parts; one part of the mind must work as a doer and other part to become witness of all doings. One part of the mind must initiate an action while another part is supposed to evaluate that very action. It is indeed as difficult as asking the tongue to check its own taste or asking eye to see itself. Enormous difficulties in bringing this clarity invite serious seekers to use their own methods where some may succeed and others fail miserably. Since 'me' and 'seer' for everyone is different from others so what works for one may not work for others.

Self is also an object by itself, the one that is witnessed or observed as an aspect present. Here it remains the basic form of consciousness, something that becomes obvious and recognizable only when maturity transcendence. This duality requires great efforts to see through. At this stage of journey of Understanding Self, our efforts need be focused on developing the cracks in the wall of this duality because those cracks alone will let us catch glimpse of things on the other side.

Process of Awakening 'Me'

The 'me' part is to be awakened by going beyond the gaze of the observer. This awakening gets facilitated by sinking the accumulated layers of shades such as useless memories, tardy traditions, rubbish rituals, apathetic teachings, endured experiences, borrowed perceptions, and everything else that prevents the right access to the genuine truth. It is here that the proverb of 'unlearning required for new learning' gets applied in its purest form. The personal identification with all negative forces like despair, conflicts, competitions, comparisons, aggressions, violence, attachments, failures need to be completely ended by seeing through these as transient. Taking all these dilemma issues one by one, and focusing attention as an external observer, each practitioner revisits his perceived knowledge about self and replaces the same with neutral knowledge. It is like rewriting new software and replacing the old one. All types of contemplation, named meditation or otherwise are primarily used for this very re-writing.

When it comes to issues to be taken up for contemplation, it is better to include practically everything one does in daily life. Mundane activities like what you talk, think, react to, read, watch, or listen, are to be made subject of contemplation process one by one. You better cover everything flashing through your mind without differentiating anything as big or small, significant or otherwise, important or useless. You should observe smallest of detail like each word used in all types of communications, intentions going through the mind, motives coming out of mental processes, fears, dreams, aspirations, people and feelings igniting hate and love, indifferences towards something or someone and reasons thereof, things that you wish to acquire, things that you wish to hold or dispense with. Idea is to develop sharper but neutral view to observe and understand the result as it appears, without any coloring or justification or judgment. This is certainly a long-drawn process demanding tons of patience and dedication.

Sinking of this baggage of colored layers brings newly found freedom for the self, allowing it to regain its original nature filled with innocence, love and peace. In a way, the entire communication narrated in the Bhagwat Gita is extension of this very process where Arjuna is 'me' and faced with dilemma and lord Krishna is the aim of human life. All the methods and approaches discussed in all of 18 chapters of Gita are processes for facilitating that very evolution of 'me', the Arjuna, to unite with the Supreme Self, Krishna, by removing all ignorance from Arjuna's mind and prepare him to undertake his own right-full obligation without losing his access to superior aim. Every aspirant must regain the same Arjuna nature through study, practice, contemplation and more practices.

Having captured everything happening from a distance, the next step is to absorb the essence of things captured. This calls for clear differentiation between seeing and observing; while one is mechanical activity the other is qualitative. Keen observation is significantly different than fixing a gaze. More than open eyes, real seeing involves a loving heart and a mind filled with peace and tranquility. And in order to become peaceful, the mind should be ready to shed its existing inhibitions, and its judgmental nature. All you need, is to have a fresh approach, full attention, and pure perspective. Once you acquire such a state of mind, everything you see will be like seeing it for the first time. In short, the lenses used for observing must be cleaned of every particle of shade, dust or dirt. Such pure observation alone provides access to your true self.

> "The moment one gives close attention to anything, even a blade of grass, it becomes a mysterious, awesome, indescribably magnificent world in itself."
>
> — *Henry Miller*

The challenge in developing such an observation is our willingness to rise above our divided existence. Keen observation brings us in direct confrontation with ongoing cluttering in our mind which is mostly scaring in nature. But let us remember that good or ugly, whatever we observe is already a part of our life. Reality does not change or vanish simply because we decide to look aside. Train yourself as the video camera that captures everything happening irrespective of qualitative aspect of the event. A camera does its work irrespective of the event being birth or death. Camera doesn't differentiate an event being accidental or planned perfectly. Your observation must act accordingly.

The observation for self is not one time activity and need be carried as long as it takes. It is only over long periods that pure observation becomes a habit. It needs to become one's second nature. One must keep trying until such time that the real intention behind every action and thought comes out as clear as water. Please remember that at this stage, there is no fixing required. Forget fixing, we need not even conclude anything wanted or despised.

Improving observation is exactly like playing golf. You can read about it as much you like but you become comfortable on the course only after years of actual playing experience. Basically, Golf is played with yourself. You have the entire course open to you and you have bag full of clubs to hit a stationary ball that needs to be put in different holes. But in between there are factors like temperature, humidity, altitude, wind velocity, wind direction, quality of soil, length of grass etc. which have direct bearing on your game. Managing these factors require a great deal of training, practice and concentration. All these points apply to developing keen observation verbatim. Various techniques available are the clubs to be used and entire psychological space is the golf course one uses. Number of shots taken to reach the destination is the period required to reach to final goal. Finally, the role of a teacher or guide is no different than that of an experienced caddy.

For quality observation, you remind yourself that you are here to observe the reality rooted in self-experience by completely shunning all the borrowed knowledge or tutoring from others. Forget completely what has been read, known or believed until now. That was past and past does not help in developing awareness. Awareness requires the functioning of our conscious focus on present unfolding here and now. It should be like first time watching live stream of an unknown sport where there is neither any recording nor any commentary. Unwholesome tendencies involving imaginations and speculations about future also need be stopped as part of this process. Ability to blank out both past and future and holding on to present alone is the key to become aware. Let us try being aware in a practical way.

Exercise for Observing Contents of Own Mind

- Take your sitting pose as if you are sitting for meditation position and breathe deeply for a couple of minutes.
- Imagine yourself sitting alone in a movie theatre with a blank 70 mm screen in the front. At this stage close your eyes and take your focus on mental contents at that moment.
- Feel relaxed as if you are waiting for the movie to start and continue focusing on the imagined screen in keen anticipation.
- In due course, you start feeling some live video playing involving situations going through your mind and your feelings at that moment of time.
- Pay attention to the images; to sound of words being spoken, smell of the scenes, sensations aroused by the images getting flashed.
- Refrain from any desire to intervene in the happenings, just watch.
- Withhold any judgement and allow things to happen of its own.
- Take notice of change of scenes, events and actors, let them play out cool.
- After a few minutes, please come out of your experience and try recollecting what all was happening.
- Realize that things displayed were contents of your own conscious mind itself at that very moment.
- Repeat this exercise over several sittings to get acquainted with your mental contents with clarity and purpose.

The best way to develop required penetration for pure observation is to place our observing self out of our body to focus on self from a distance. Let us imagine an invisible drone fitted with camera and mind reader equipment, moving at some distance in front, to capture each one of our mental impulses. Its feedback to us, as an unattached, independent and unbiased third umpire on a cricket field with access to replay, may prove to be the best technique for exploring self. Once you focus your search at the right place, with right intent and unbiased attitude, your own intentions and underlying responses and reactions are destined to get decoded to you as an open book.

> "He who knows others is wise. He who knows himself is enlightened."
>
> —*Lao Tzu, Ancient Chinese Philosopher*

Let us now look at the contents of pure observation. In this process you are bound to come over new facts that you did not know earlier. For example, you may come across your dislike for someone or some things, you may be lacking discipline in certain activities, at times you may be behaving outside morally unacceptable norms, your intellectual strengths may not be as stronger as you believed thus far, your memory may be much poorer, your ethics may not prove as rock solid as you assumed so far, you may be jealous of some person in close vicinity. Ability to identify and face accurate answers to these questions is yet another stage to be self-aware. Right answers will remove the opaqueness from your persona and allow right clarity and purity to inner space. Knowing everything about self and knowing it accurately, is the purpose of entire self-awareness drive.

Embrace Reality without Fear

Pure observation on all scattered parts of life can broadly be grouped into two simple but important brackets, that is, fears and pleasures. With improved self-exploration and focused observation, we can see these pleasures and fears along with underlying reasons. For example, awareness about fears forces us to escape from situations and increases our dependence on others. Some of those are in our close relations while many others are from external world. Some of these people come to us and many others that we go to. Soon this list of people we depend on becomes long enough. But this dependence, like every other dependence, starts inhibiting our freedom and we do not even realize it. The real physical or psychological fears are far and few. Most of these are based on repetitive thoughts relating to 'what will happen if....' syndrome.

Pleasures also meet the similar fate. Every time we experience something nice, our brain records those events on its hard disc. As a natural tendency, thoughts keep going back to those experiences and we continue desiring for their repetitions. Both fears and pleasures are dependent on thoughts. Now thoughts are also used for almost every other human activity like speaking, making scientific discoveries, managing all our past impressions. We cannot do without strong thinking process functioning rationally, logically and objectively. On physical level, thoughts get generated based on inputs from body's sense organs and characterization of that feedback by the mind and we know that our body has many marvelous sensing devices capable of sensing even subtle variations. But characterization of all such inputs is done by mind under influence of past knowledge and experiences. Letting the mind to break such characterization is called creative imagination, which is largely operated by intuitive guidance. Old experiences seldom lead to creative imagination, a faculty so critical for bringing unique solutions and results.

Creative imagination works best under intuitive guidance, the ability to acquire knowledge without inference. Intuition helps us know the reality in a flash. Ideas out of intuition are every time rated above ideas using intellect. Interestingly, when used as a servant, human mind honors every request made to it by intuitive guidance. In this mode, the mind is willingly engaged in learning. That is how all inventions and creations come into existence.

How to improve your intuition? There are specific initiatives suggested for the purpose. Firstly, practice making your mind quiet in order to listen inner voice. Regularly experiencing silence and frequently getting into natural settings are known ways of making the mind quiet. Calming of mind is also helped by practicing breathing exercises or meditation techniques you prefer. You should also learn to trust your hunches and gut feeling. This can be practiced making self your playmate and play guessing games. Intuition is not God gifted and is always earned by practice.

Management of Thoughts

The next key point is to manage thoughts. Incidentally, developed intuitive guidance comes very handy in managing thoughts. When our mind gets occupied with learning, it is known to quickly replace its earlier impressions. So, engaging the mind in continuous learning, both voluntary and induced, is the most effective process for managing thoughts.

> "The mind is by nature restless. Begin liberating it from its restlessness; give it peace; make it free from distractedness; make this a habit. This can be done by ignoring the external world and removing the obstacles to peace of mind."
>
> — *Ramana Maharshi*

After developing keen observation our intelligence need be tuned to apply findings in a neutral way. Soon, thoughts motivated by intuitive guidance react with our intelligence and motivate the mind to learn something it was not ready to do earlier. Beyond this stage, ours 'being human' helps as the logical reasoning prompts human brain to set right anything it finds problem with. We are programmed like that, and no special efforts are required to activate this impulse. The resistance to change stands only until we are not convinced that something is wrong in the first place. Finally, a mind that starts learning is destined to enhance its own intelligence. This is the turning point for subsequent journey paving way for bringing all desired improvements at all levels.

Once we are well aware of our actions in real life, we take control of all our initiatives and reactions by making logical choices based on unbiased, unconditioned and un-fragmented new learning in place of our attitudes, behaviours, emotions and feelings used earlier. When clear observation and enhanced awareness ignite the generation of creative thoughts, the same mind is directed to learn and take well-informed actions. Right actions in turn result in right emotions and feelings as well.

Events and people from external world remain active even now and they do impact life as before but our response to such actions now is qualitatively different. Actions by others will no longer trigger our emotions. Emotions are chemical molecules that act as command circuits in our body. Once our newfound skill of being self-aware can put stop to activation of the said circuits, emotions stop interfering with our actions. That stops igniting our fears or pleasures. What happens now is fresh processing of keen observation conveyed to mind without any connectivity with the old baggage.

> "The thoughts resolve themselves. Just sit there with them. The reason they don't get resolved is because you're either running away or fighting them. If you sit there with something long enough, it will get resolved." — Naval Ravikant

4

Pathways for Understanding Self

Having absorbed the scope, significance and spectrum of the process of understanding self, let us now change gears and work on second and more important aspect of advancement of self. First of all, let us begin discussing various suggestions and recommendations made by contemporary scholars and thinkers relating to surface level suggestions directly implementable by any present-day adult. Points enumerated hereunder may not appear important to advance self directly as these are similar to preparing ground before planting a sapling. Efforts to grow best of plant in a ground full of pebbles, litter and rubbish are destined to offer only partial gains irrespective of how much watering and manuring get applied. Being direct and visible, these are simpler to implement and offer opportunity to measure benefits flowing at comparatively faster pace. Being general in nature but significant in character, these bring positive results in all spheres of life.

Suggested Pathways

A. Do not Judge Everything Around

Pronouncing judgement over the smallest of issues is a serious business. A judge goes through lots of testimonies, arguments, counter arguments, cross-examinations, and a whole lot of evidence evaluation before delivering his judgement. Facts are studied, evidence are corroborated and verified, then alone the judgement is passed. Pronouncing a ruling casually invariably leads to defective judgements. But if one is to take a pause for a moment and assimilate situations in real life, it will be seen that quite inadvertently we often pass judgements, in a very causal manner, at the drop of hat.

We take offence to small things people do and misinterpret words spoken by others. We get touchy if our opinions are not taken by people in inner circle or when our opinion get sidelined. This list of situations where we conclude things happening in manner that we do not approve, can go on and on. At times, we also come to quick conclusions without any logic. For example, fifteen minutes into a movie, and we give ruling that story line is not impressive, or direction is weak, or the acting of leads is lifeless. One can spot normal life situations which are clear instances of actions qualifying as rulings by a self-appointed judge. We want everybody else to do things in the way that matches our liking. Your mind can justify as why you feel the way you feel and how you came to your conclusions, but it goes without saying that such pronouncements are just inadvertently passed judgments.

Be cognizant that you do not know well about others and their situation to judge their actions and words. Also, that one person's right may be another person's wrong. Eyes get deceived, ears listen only partial truth, and testimony of third parties are found wrong all the time. How many times in past your impressions about others were found wrong? How many times you regretted your reactions being hasty or being out of place? How many times you regretted speaking wrong words resulting in repenting later on?

You are responsible only for yourselves alone. Accept words and actions of others as given. It is not so hard to consider them as their best and echo them with your best. This simple harmless principle has power to significantly reduce most of day-to-day problems arising from interactions with others. The moment we firmly refuse to stand as judge for matter of others, a whole lot of ugliness, pettiness, shallowness and selfishness disappear from life.

So, every time you get an impulse to take sides, control yourself. Please handover the matter to your logical mind and let it ponder what needs to be done, that is, if at all there is a thing to be done by you. Tell your ego to rest and let the judgements be delivered by actual judges. Make your delay devices stronger than before to avoid enumerable extempore assertions. This is very significant for making the mind still and gaining peace. Desire to detest from passing judgements contributes to mind's willingness for yielding to focus inward.

B. Stop Short of Self-Deception

Humans are masters of self-deception. People constantly deceive themselves without even realizing it. The tendency for self-deception stems from the simple and genuine desire to leave a better impression on others around. There are other reasons for doing that too. As a definition, 'self-deception involves a person who seems to acquire and maintain some false belief in the teeth of evidence to the contrary because of some motivation, and who may display behavior suggesting some awareness of the truth'.

Much of the empirical work on biased self-evaluations has explored the motivation for overestimating our own abilities or viewing ourselves as better than we truly are. This motivation is so strong that most people ignore or rationalize negative information about themselves to maintain a positive self-image. They use motivated reasoning to interpret ambiguous information in ways that confirm their generally positive beliefs and attitudes about themselves. We can also see them displaying imposing creativity in justifying their acts of deception. Self-deception is clear violation of honesty as a value. As we know, honesty is not just about telling the truth. It is about being real with our self and others about who we are, what we want and what we need, to live our most authentic life. Honesty sharpens our perception and allows us to observe everything around us with clarity.

The most important way to determine whether you are lying or not is to observe yourself, without judgment or evaluation. Ultimately, there will be a situation when self-deceivers will have to face reality. After all, deception cannot continue forever. It is said that self-deception diminishes over time when self-deceivers are repeatedly confronted with evidence of their reality. However, even this learning is unable to remove their susceptibility for future self-deceptions. Just notice and start asking questions that can reveal your internal motivations. As you do this, focus on three areas:

1. ***Take note of your emotions*** – It is established that if a person remained burdened by some painful, raw or unresolved issues, he tends to over-react emotionally to other issues and people as well. As and when you come across a strong emotional reaction to something or someone, you are best advised to take a pause and contemplate quietly about the reason of such emotional reaction. You must be sure to pinpoint if the present reaction is caused by new situation or it is getting triggered because of some carry over burden from past.

2. *Take notice of your thoughts* – Surely, we would love a situation where our thoughts are always based on reflection of reality and not on some non-existent imaginary. Beyond desire, people normally believe that their thoughts are true and right. Little they realize that their thoughts are peculiarly inaccurate, imperfect and often ill-founded on beliefs than reality. Our inaccurate thinking reflects painful realities that we just do not want to admit. Given this reality, when we notice our thinking going into extremes or becoming irrational, we should again take a little break and fact check and self-inquire about accuracy of thoughts.

You can start even in baby steps by taking few gentle deep breaths in a space of your choice and later shift your attention to your thinking process. Knowing that you are not what your thoughts are and that there is no need to believe what you think, is always a good beginning. Just because it is yours, you don't have to get imprisoned by your thoughts. This process is later explained as meditation.

3. *Keep an eye on your behavior* – Many people desperately want their behavior to be different from their identity. People do not want to believe that their actions result in showing who they really are. It is natural to cover for wrong actions as abrasions and ignore them as desired exceptions. For example, one may not admit that he is basically jealous or suspicious type even though he often checks his significant other's phone messages and social media posts through fake id. The truth is that our behavior reflects who we are in more ways than one. Every time, our behavior is not in line of what we want, there is a reason for us to step back for a while and ask a question 'Why am I acting like this? Or, what is the ignition point of such poor behavior? Is there a thing that I do not want to admit to myself about my behavior? By observing your emotions, thoughts, and behaviors, you can learn about who you really are and give yourselves the opportunity to change.

There is another important side to self-deception, and it pertains to its impact of others around. We must appreciate that we cannot be honest with others until we first are honest with ourselves. When we deceive ourselves, we often burden and damage our relationships as well. Let us remind our self that being honest requires deliberate and consistent effort on a daily basis. We know that to appear convincing we should be fully convinced. Every person is surer about self when they do things moral and selfless. Reverse also is equally true. You do a thing that is morally questionable, and you cannot avoid feeling alienated from yourself. As such, in the end, self-deception does not work.

C. Practice Sadhana on Daily basis

Sadhana can be defined in many ways, but for the limited purpose at present, let us look at it as a daily purification practice aimed at self-enrichment by undertaking regular exercises of self-inquiry. Unlike worship, sadhana is conducted to please no one but to churn, brainstorm or shake your own understanding of all practical issues. Sadhana is the process of separating butter from creamy curd. Because basically we all are human beings having real life experiences, we must sit out daily for reflecting over our actions with ultimate purpose of bringing changes wherever required. Sadhana is required daily to clear all dust gathering on the mirror of our hearts and minds. With dust around, the best of mirror remains unable to reflect the reality with clarity. Daily Sadhana is arguably the best practice to clear your consciousness so that you are able to connect with your conscience, your infinite self.

Some sources consider sadhana in a very wide spectrum and include recitation of mantras, sitting in specific asanas, going for particular kriya, or even reading of scriptures. But for our specific purpose in hand, Sadhana is to be used as a daily exercise for self-inquiry to reprocess all undesirable thoughts, actions or behaviors disturbing mental peace on that day and finally, once all such issues get resolved, to ponder upon spiritual existence. In that sense, Sadhana stands apart from meditation. The focus under Sadhana, in limited scope being applied here, is on immediate or just concluded day(s) and idea is to constantly purify thoughts, words and actions rather than very long term and spiritual horizon touched by meditation. Sadhana offer wider choice over tools and techniques and provides liberty of even becoming much more experimental as against meditation where certain degree of structured approach is strongly recommended.

D. Realize Your Modesty

"Everyone thinks of changing the world, but no one thinks of changing himself."

— Leo Tolstoy

We should realize our modesty and keep reminding ourselves that we have only so little role to play on this stage called human life. Our individual identity is important to only us, immediate family, few friends, even fewer coworkers, customers, or clients. Indeed, a person lives his life in a very small piece of the world and interacts with very few people. So, know yourself fully and try improving your identity within the sphere of your tiny world and don't worry too much about others. It is enough to live your life and bring some improvement if you can within your own self and immediate community you are part of and enjoy it.

Let us realize that there is no point in controlling destinies of others including children, spouse, employees, associates, and every other person touching our life in some or the other way. Let others take their own decisions, take lead in their initiatives and celebrate their life as they deem fit. As soon as you accept your modesty genuinely, a whole lot of mental agony disappears within moments, and of its own. This realization always leads to impressive progress in self exploration process. It is best to polish your own unused skills because, for sure, there are many uncut/unpolished diamonds lying deep down in your internal pockets waiting to be discovered. You are best advised to focus on converting those very stones into gems.

E. Say Bye-bye to Haste and Impulsiveness

Haste keeps the mind occupied and kills possibilities for its willful surrender to withdraw from external world and focus on inside. Hurry also leaves no room for frequent inward reflections, unarguable essence of self-exploration. As scientifically proven by famous American cardiologists Meyer Friedman and Ray Rosenman, remaining in hurry is a full-blown sickness with noticeable symptoms waiting to be diagnosed and treated. They coined a new term "Hurry Sickness" as an ongoing struggle and continuous attempt to accomplish or achieve more and more things or participate in more and more events in less and less time. People with hurry sickness think fast, talk fast, and act fast.

Let us remember that people approaching life without hurry enjoy their present and preserve vigor to live a grand life in future. We must also realize that the years of working life are higher than years of post-retirement. Even when the lifespan is increasingly going up, so is the case for working life. And most people keep postponing enjoyment and relaxation for post-retirement stage without even realizing that pacing up too much results in reduction of life span itself. There are practical cases where we see people spending health to earn money and in early retirement years itself forced to spend that money for securing health.

Let us aspire to have loving and respecting individuals around, enjoying natural health and vitality. We should surely wish to grow on many fronts simultaneously but let us resolve to make these attempts with our calmness and happiness intact. Well, all this is possible once we learn and practice to slow down and take our foot away from the accelerator pedal of our life. Then alone we might have chance to enjoy the beautiful surroundings on either side while we remain in journey called life.

F. Make Simplicity your Philosophy of Life

We make countless choices every single day. Each choice ignites new options for many more choices, and the process continues. We must have a well thought out philosophy in place to deal with multiple options because future is built on those choices. Simplicity is that very philosophy and had guided millions over centuries to live good life without pressures and preferences. Simplicity is a foundational Eastern value. Besides being easy and effortless, it indirectly helps in overcoming desires and attachments. It is not to be confused with minimalism which is certainly an outdated and impractical approach in today's time. In modern times, you cannot live normal life with minimalism, but principle of simplicity is Sanatana, eternal in character, and is as relevant today as it was ever and will remain so in times to come as well.

Simplicity implies beauty, purity and clarity. Simplicity is practical and pragmatic. It leads to self-sufficiency. Simplicity must be an obvious way for everyone as it keeps complexities and complications at bay. Why we fail to believe in this virtue, well simply because its opponent, the consumerism got higher visibility. Consumerism is so visible and loud that people are unable to see the damages it incurs to our pockets and mental peace. Its severe adverse impact on environment failed to come to surface for a long period. It is only in recent years that it became a talking point among policy makers and academia.

Consumerism has simply converted present day majority into its slaves. In simple words, consumerism involves acquiring material things, owning them, using them and keeping them on display for others to notice and appreciate. In addition to material possessions, there is another form of consumerism in terms of psychological distractions through lifestyle choices. This is equally fatal and one need to guard against. Be it entertainment, social media interactions, experiences, news feeds, holidays and even relationships, for people suffering from consumerism, material enjoyment is at the center.

Another enemy of simplicity is our ego. As seen, ego strongly believes and thrives on uniqueness, which is just opposite of simplicity. Simplicity celebrates unity and oneness, but Ego takes pride in projecting us someone special, someone totally different from all others. Being part of a crowd, is never liked by ego. Little it realizes that simplicity is greatest form of sophistication. Another villain standing against simplicity is less discussed but completely malignant in nature is intellectualism. People indulging in justifying their complex actions must not forget that over-intellectualism is a sure sign of complication. Every kind of manipulation, justification and fabrication in action means poor simplicity getting sacrificed at open altar.

How can we practice simplicity? Simple approach is to start believing in things like 'I don't know' or 'it is ok' or 'let it be'. Starting with these easy to implement baby steps is by itself a strong beginning to avoid complexities. No one needs to know all the things, after all. Similarly, saying a clear and straightforward 'no' guards against many possible complexities. 'No' is much stronger a word than most other two letter words in entire English dictionary. It has great potential, and its use offers many solutions. It is a proven antidote against unreasonable demands and unrealistic expectations.

Simplicity fundamentally is a state of mind rather than a standard of living. Simplicity is grounded on sense of fairness and equity. Simplicity fosters harmonious relations among everyone around.

Let us quickly look at some useful tips to practice simplicity on day-to-day basis.

1. Prepare a list of things you need before you leave for the market. Refuse to pick up anything outside your list.
2. Develop the habit of sorting things that are no more required. Unknowingly, people keep holding things like birthday gifts,.
3. Learn and practice the art of giving away. Everything useless for you may have use for someone else. You need to make efforts to identify them and donate as often as possible..
4. Keep the use of gadgets to minimum. Gadgets are addictive and bring unavoidable complexities.
5. Enjoy things without owning them; for example, one can make use of public libraries, gardens, pools, parks, gyms. Many other things are best used on hire. You carry no responsibility to maintain and pay only when you actually use it.
6. Getting connected with nature is the simplest way of living simply. Try spending more time outdoors, go for regular walks and treks, nurture the nature, and appreciate blessings on offer by nature.

7. Become debt free and remain debt free.
8. Use selected words for honest speech. Refuse to say a word unless you meant it. Develop habit of taking a small pause before replying even during your normal communications. Little time taken can do wonders for right selection of word and protect you from contributing to avoidable misunderstandings.
9. Be fair to everything and everyone. Don't expect favors, neither give them to others. Stand tall against oppressions of all types. If nothing else, this goes to improve self-respect in your own eyes.
10. Seek love, justice and peace, foremost. If anything distracts you from that purpose, let it go.

G. Attain Internal Silence

The word silence here is being used as the nearest translation for Sanskrit word 'Mauna' which, in Hindu philosophy is said to have a voice of its own and is largely referred to peace of mind, the inner quietude. Actually, we must remain focused on silence of mind much more than outer verbal silence. Continuously speaking through thoughts is much bigger a problem for our purpose than abstaining from speaking words out of mouth. The reason for this is because thoughts are more erratic, disturbing, over emotional or out of control. So, reader is advised to comprehend right meaning conveyed by 'silence' every time the word gets used throughout this explanation. Going a step further, Ramana Maharishi equates Mauna to state of Egolessness, where mind is firmly established in heart and primal thought of "I" disappears for the thought of ever-existing real self. This very silence is the real silence we are looking.

"The quieter you become, the more you are able to hear." — Rumi

Silence relaxes the brain and opens doors for genuine imagination, basic intuition and original thinking. Phenomenal psychological and emotional health benefits are just other incidental benefits of practising silence. Silence also helps reducing doubts and guides us correctly to take decisions under tight situations.

For exploration of self, more importantly, we have to achieve silence from resonance and reverberations of logic, internal arguments, internal debates, never ending evaluations, comparisons, and mental chattering. We also have to deal with noise of ongoing monologues, running stories of triumphs and defeats, past failures and future fears, current pressures and anxieties. Even when we do not realize, all these enemies of silence keep us disturbed much more than higher decibels. Most importantly, internal noise that we have to guard against, comes from multiple sources listed below. It is critical to take note of all these sources before you hope to make desired progress:

- Cries of Emotions and Feelings
- Uproars of Desires and Passions
- Voice of Faiths and Beliefs
- Rattling of Attitudes and Prejudices
- Clamoring of Fears and Anxieties
- Yelling of Ego

- Murmuring of Opinions and Judgements
- Detonation of Habits and Obsessions
- Hissing Sounds of Doubts and Suspicions

This list clearly expands the scope and significance of silence to its real comprehension. Sounds from all these dimensions keep our mind agitated even when we are all alone, inside our cozy homes, sleeping in night on well secured beds. So much so that these forces do not allow us to even dream peacefully. Our very existence is indeed noisy. These sources of noise overwhelm our ability to listen inside voice. It is critical to discuss and take care of above enemies of silence simply because the moment we talk about silence our intelligent but ignorant mind starts jumping to blame uncontrollable environmental sources leaving aside more lethal and comparatively controllable internal issues aside.

Agreed that silence is too feeble and every human effort to pursue, protect and promote interest of every kind ends up breaking silence. Actually, life itself is a form of noise and it is almost impossible to avoid it. On the other hand, every quest for salvation necessitates access to complete silence. Practising silence is a personal and optional choice. Expertise to use silence effectively is a sure sign of wisdom of the beholder. Connection with our inner silence allows us to see through our real hurts and wounds. That clarity later enables us to attend to the curses. And because when you know better you deal better, acknowledging them lead to finding cure for curses.

> "*To make the right choices in life, you have to get in touch with your soul. To do this, you need to experience silence, which most people are afraid of, because in the silence you hear the truth and know the solutions.*" — Deepak Chopra

Practice for silence requires erecting strong barriers to filter minutest content before allowing it to enter into your mental space. Reconnecting to our pure silence is a sure way to minimize external stimuli and internal chirping.

> "*Fools disagree due to ignorance. Intelligent disagree due to excess knowledge. Wise neither agree nor disagree but remain silent. That is why he is called Mauni, the silent one.*"

H. Transpose Old Learning with New Wisdom

A mind unwilling to learn is a dumb mind as it remains engrossed on past impressions. Such a mind is lazy and works only for justifying what it knows already. It considers old knowledge sufficient. But world is changing fast. New scenarios are getting scripted for almost everything. We have to keep pace to learn new things evolving on fast pace. But success in learning depends on the intensity of the passion with which it is pursued. Learning is not limited by education, age, experience or such other known constraints. A learning mind remains a fresh mind and makes every experience exciting.

Learning is never constrained for scope. It is like expansion of space that the more you know, more you realize how little you knew before. It is a never-ending process and one life is too less a period for this. Learning through reading is considered a good habit. Reading is a skill worth acquiring and the easiest of tools to learn more with lesser efforts. Throwing your towel by saying that 'I am not into reading' is a sign of your mind fooling you. Mind needs to be told in no unclear words that it is obliged to read and retain the content of every good material it gets exposed to. Reading connects you with the wisdom of others in the fastest possible way. But reading must be the real reading. Picking up a book and simply flipping through its pages with the intention of reaching to the end does not qualify as real reading. Authors dealing with significant subjects basically carve out their life's learning in the form of their books or blogs. Selection of your reading material is your exclusive prerogative, and you have every right not to pick up a book. You are also within your rights to fold the book in between if you find it digressing from your expectations. But so long as you are reading, you ought to remain hospitable for its content as well as its intent.

True reading requires a sharp focus to grasp the knowledge contained in the writing. You must read the lines as well as in between the lines. If you read without focus, your efforts of reading will fail to fire your imaginations. Objective reading requires very open and slow approach to facilitate sinking of new knowledge up to right depth. The focus should be to chew the words and sentences until every drop of delicious juices contained therein are extracted in full. Let the knowledge conveyed by words sink in your conscious mental space without any ambiguity. Let us remember that words must travel the distance from mind to heart before they really become ours. Physically that may appear a very short distance, but it is full of long-lasting detours and sinkholes which, at times, prove too long a distance.

Other than reading from books, there are four other established sources of gaining knowledge. These are – intuition, authority, rational induction and finally empiricism. As already explained earlier, intuition get activated with purity of knowledge gained through gut feeling. You have to wait for it rather than learning it to emerge. Authority refers to gaining knowledge from parents, teachers, or other people having more experience than us. Speaking normally, learning through books explained above fall under this source only. Rational induction refers to the source of learning through reasoning and proofs. It starts by assuming something and later arranging proof to prove the same. It is more like cause and effect method where you gather past knowledge and make use of that in others contexts. Empiricism, on the other hand, is knowledge gained through careful observation, manipulation of variables through the scientific method, repeating research designs, and taking in data to interpret. Empiricism is the accepted role of knowledge in psychological research because psychologists use statistics and believe in probabilistic conclusion. We should explore all possible sources of gaining new learnings and ensure personal growth at all times.

I. Make Peace with your Emotions

Emotions influence our feelings, thinking, actions and responses on moment-to-moment basis. Emotions are part of our system of sensing and responding to the entire world and differentiate human beings from robots. Significant overarching impact of emotions on our life demands deeper understanding, appreciating their interplay and finally ability to exercise regulation so that merit of our actions and responses is not lost. Emotional imbalance means ongoing tug of war between heart and mind. It means your logical side and emotions are at odds with each other. You cannot think of connecting with your core under such situation. More so that emotions are very pragmatic and audacious; they keep reappearing in our system even after years of working on them. Regulating them is always tricky and a lifelong challenge.

Wisdom lies in learning the art of managing emotions without involving other people. Mastery in this art also give a big boost to all critical sense of self-worth. Again, it is very important to appreciate that suppression, denying, intensifying, weakening, curtailing, masking or replacing powers of emotions are options that may sound good but are completely impractical and are bound to fail every time.

Emotions are critically important because they hold key to our feelings, thinking, and actions on a moment-to-moment basis. Bigger the swing of emotions, larger is the level of anxiety. Ability to acquire emotional balance depends on moral and ethical preparations, evolved self-awareness together with identifying real purpose of human life. This also calls for perfecting acceptance for every person, objects and situations around as given. One must be able to filter and let go everything outside individual control. All these initiatives, however, give results in bit-by-bit manner, in the continuous circle of learning, practicing and perfecting in baby steps. Regulating emotions in nothing short of discarding the original skills one has lived with for ages.

Reaching to our deepest core requires good functioning of our emotional immune systems which in turn requires higher self-esteem at work. By maintaining arm's length distance with our emotions, we empower our rational mind to remain in control. That is how we gain right power to deal with common psychological assaults being thrown by normal life every now and then. On the other hand, if we allowed negative emotions to remain in stream, they remain capable of hijacking our frontal lobes, our brain's architecture, leaving us in a heightened stress-response state. These are all ripe conditions for halting out connection with our core.

Positive emotions, on the other hand, are essential for proper thinking, problem solving, and focused attention. Since understanding self do require a lot of new learning, it is necessary to maintain balance of our emotions.

J. Enhance Compassion Quotient

The word compassion being used here is in context of Indian words of "Daya", "Karuna", "Anukampa" and "Kripa", all rolled into one. Each of these words singularly as well as collectively represent desire to extend your shoulder to mitigate the sorrows and miseries of others. Please recall the combined strength of all these words every time you see the word Compassion being used under this explanation. It is much beyond a normal likable value and actually extend to become an all-inclusive and deeply interconnected humanity where you feel for everyone around at par with your own self. You can also look at compassion as a state of mind where there is no trace of ill-will of any kind for anyone. Thoughts of harming others or actual violence of any sort, stand much smaller in comparison to compassion. Here you desire others to gain freedom from all their difficulties, sufferings or oppressions. The most critical role of compassion is to weaken the all important ego, one of the most tedious obstacle on way to exploring your own depth in right light.

Compassion does wonders in bringing peace with everything around. It celebrates the mutual connectivity rooted on Sanatan principle of equity and sharing. Most importantly, the affinity desired for practicing compassion is based on genuine sense of belonging and togetherness rather than any benevolence being shown by those 'having' for those 'not having'. Once compassion get firmly rooted right up to behavior and attitude levels, it contributes to help bring down all walls existing between friends or enemies alike. It enables you to deal with every one in similar fashion without any differentiation of any kind.

It also helps in shaking strings of attachments with persons or things earlier operating under desire to control or to seek love/affection in return. Disappearance of attachments helps in evaporating biases, partialities or associations. Fully developed compassion allows you to establish associations with strong sense of equality and commonality. This leads to chain reaction bringing end to fears and anxieties and augmentation of positive qualities of kindness, generosity and tolerance, and all these bring us much closer to our deeper core.

> *"A mind committed to compassion is like an overflowing reservoir – a constant source of energy, determination and kindness. Or this can be likened to a seed; when cultivated, it gives rise to many qualities, such as, tolerance, inner strength, and confidence to overcome fear and insecurity."* — Anonymous

K. Spend Time in Solitude

> *"My yearning is my cup, my burning thirst is my drink, and my solitude is my intoxication; I do not and shall not quench my thirst. But in this burning that is never extinguished is a joy that never wanes".* — Khalil Gibran

Solitude, as being discussed here, mean much more than being physically alone. Solitude is being in a state where one can park worldly baggage in a separate space and allow the body to perfectly catch up with mind without the burden of any baggage whatsoever. Spending time in solitude is critical for freedom from distractions. Solitude helps in concentrating focus on a subject of choice. Most importantly, solitude enables our brain to think outside the box and come up with unique solutions. Time spent in solitude runs counter to the norms of being social. Spending some time away from the hustle and bustle of society ultimately proves beneficial for every person interested in exploring Self.

Ancient Indian traditions also acclaim solitariness and consider it as a precondition for spiritual wellbeing and achieving enlightenment. Thinking loudly, the two critical stages of vanaprastha and sannyasa, which cover full second half of human expected life, are nothing but two distinct stages of living life in solitude. People like us living in modern times need not follow ancient traditions because the entire scenarios of living life is so much different now. We will, however, do better by creating solitude corners within our private space and spend time there as often as possible. Let us agree that modern living is full of over stimulations and mind needs to suspend its over-activism for as long as feasible. Let us look at solitude as anti-adrenaline therapy that kicks on when there is no danger of fight-or-flight response, the principle which helped humanity survive during its early days. Solitude helps us feel deep connect with the entire creation in a timeless and spaceless realm where soul feels at home and heart enjoys its quivering.

Success in exploring Self calls for proficiency to swim against the tides. A mind can develop that ability only when it remains free from all types of compulsions and pressures. For this purpose, you are advised to get yourself bored rather than loaded with activities. Please find regular occasions when you have nothing to do. Cellular phones, TV, newspapers, social media, internet, books, thoughts, sports, social engagements, entertainments, to do list etc. are all essential, but not always. Persistent switching from one engagement to another is neither good for happiness nor for spiritual growth. Activity less boredom is the recharging time that does wonders to creativity by germinating seeds of self-discovery. Solitude is must for contemplating big questions in our life. Solitude helps our body to catch up with mind thus balancing the 'doshas' as prescribed by Ayurveda. Solitude keeps distractions at bay and does wonders towards enhancing creativity.

> *"To make the right choices in life, you have to get in touch with your soul. To do this, you need to experience solitude, which most people are afraid of, because in the silence you here the truth and know the solutions."* — Deepak Chopra

Solitude demands periods of personal time away from mails, internet, messages, mobile phones and every other social media platform. Let us not forget that all these time-consuming activities cropped up only in last couple of decades. Humanity has survived millions of years of its history without these Gadgets and Apps. What is the use of connecting with the world on moment-to-moment basis but not connecting with self for months and years? More importantly, you need not step out of four walls of your own crowded house for any hilltop or for a boat on the sea or for a cave in the mountain, as you can enjoy blessed solitude well within your home. Loosening of attachment with the members of the family and letting them live their own life, is good enough to practice solitude. All you need is a sacred corner for a defined length of time all to yourself.

Spend time in solitude and come out of influence from external pressures. When you focus inside, you suffer less from distractions and false impressions. And most importantly, inward focus becomes possible unlike usual resistance, opposition or after-effects.

> *"The mind that is alone is not only innocent but young—not in time or age, but young, innocent, alive at whatever age— and only such a mind can see that which is truth and that which is not measurable by words."* — Jiddu Krishnamurti

Contemporary Tips for Shining Self

As the name itself suggests, Contemporary Tips are prepositions recommended by psychologists of modern era. Modern Psychology focusses on understanding individuals and groups by establishing general principles through research carried out with tests, surveys, interviews, medical evaluations, observational data, and other records. Considering their processes and research methodologies, it is fair to conclude that modern psychology provides a sound basis for its efficacy. Modern Psychology has multiple branches dedicated to specific areas of specialization. For example, Biological Psychology studies brain circuitry and biological processes covering how we act, think and feel. Behavioral Psychology focusses on how certain behaviors are learned and reinforced while Cognitive Psychology studies person's beliefs, desires, ideas, knowledge and motivations.

In terms of comparison of Self Discovery with school based formal education, the contemporary tools are like senior school education where focus is essentially on academic and cultural foundational knowledge and skill. Conformity is heavily rewarded. Testing is frequent but covers only small amounts of courses studied. The markings are fairly predictable and liberal where there are possibilities to secure near perfect scores. Students operate in fairly known environment with many friends and guides being available at back and call. But this level prepares a student to develop interest and go for specialization based on his preference and capabilities. The academic programs are rather predetermined with a limited choice for electives or optional subjects. Extra curriculum activities are largely for fun. As a guiding principle, you are expected to learn only from prescribed textbooks or material assigned by teachers. All above points are applicable to the tips getting suggested under this chapter. Recommendations grouped together here cover wide areas and that is why the number of tips provided below, in first look, may appear too many in numbers. While a particular reader may have his own reservations, questions, concerns, or maybe some apprehensions, but in general, all these recommendations apply to all modern time individuals with normal behavior in toto.

In today's time, psychological tests are commonly conducted to identify characteristics of individual's personality. Attitudes, emotions, thoughts, and behavioral traits contributing one's personality, can now be easily evaluated and used for drawing right conclusions using personality tests. These tests help determine a person's strengths and weaknesses, allowing him to make informed life choices based on his traits analysis. In particular, anyone having specific symptoms of social withdrawal, problems with thinking, decreased functioning, apathy, disconnected feelings, increased sensitivity, mood changes, unusual behavior, changes in sleep or appetite, irrational thinking, and anxiety or paranoia, must necessarily opt for a proper psychological evaluation and get benefited. That is why, now that the treatments are available, even when some of the readers might assume themselves fully fit and showing no obvious issues or symptoms requiring use of psychological studies, it is advisable to go for consultations and psychoanalysis, if and when, any symptom emerges.

The recommendations listed below are very practical and provide ways to know yourself in realistic manner. While no body denies that we need to observe ourselves in neutral manner by holding the third person's perspective, these steps just enumerate the ways for developing that very neutral approach, the "how" part of the equation. Also, these steps provide examples from actual life where there is no conceptual affiliation or belief issues. Apparently, these may not necessarily be focused on understanding self alone as these are definitely aimed at peeling off our artificial armor of assumptions and notions that may have unknowingly become integral part of normal life. To that extent, these pointers help bringing in added clarity which proves useful in several practical ways beside introducing ourselves with real we.

Before expanding these recommendations one by one, let us prepare our mind to become open and willing for trying these initiatives. Please give yourself permission to succeed and insulate from fears or doubts from opinion of others. Also, please surround yourself with positive reinforcement by remembering that subconscious mind, the part in charge for making it happen, is generally programmed to mimic and mirror what you have been doing in the past. So, do consider its resistance as perfectly natural and normal. Mind is said to have a mind of its own and it loves to behave like a master every time you expect it to be a humble servant. So, all you need to begin with is its active willingness; its voluntarily becoming ready to divert attention from outside to inside. This willingness to learn will certainly help you gain new knowledge and develop skills to help you improve your all-round performance. Please remember that a person demonstrating willingness for new learning is typically ahead for searching new opportunities and remaining ahead of normal trends.

1. Go for Objective Assessments

Taking some objective assessment test qualify as the first thing to gain greater understanding of yourself. Biggest obstacle on this path is the wrong assumption that I know myself fully and there is nothing new possible to know. Saying that I do not know myself as much I would like to, is a good beginning point. In normal situations, you may go and ask people closer to you, but their experience of you will lead them to share their biases about you. That may not be the best way to get right assessment. Getting some objective opinions, based on well-researched and well documented scientific methods certainly provides you a more accurate picture and is expected to let you to know many things you didn't know about yourself.

There are several established tests that can be taken to learn about the different aspects of yourself. The Myers-Briggs Personality type theory says that all people have 1 of 16 different basic personalities. These personalities can predict how you interact with people, the kinds of interpersonal problems and strengths that you have, and what kind of environment you live and work at your best. A basic version of this test can be found even online.

If you are struggling to understand what makes you happy and what you should do with your life, consider taking a career test. Considering your personality and what you do for fun, such tests help you know about your best options to feel satisfied on the job. There are lots of different ones available online, usually for free. But if you are in school or college you can probably get a more reputable test administered through designated career counselor. You do not stand to lose a thing here. There is absolutely no reason not to make use of available expertise of specialists. There is a theory that every person learns and processes their experience of the world in one of many ways. This is called your "learning style". Knowing your own learning style is not limited to school level education. Learning is a passion which needs to be sustained lifelong. It is never too late to learn new things. Testing your learning style help you understand why you struggle with some activities and excel at others.

Just a word of caution, please be aware that this is still an evolving science, with many theories about how many learning styles exist, and you may get different results depending on which test you take. You may also come across some controversies or negative reports about some tests which is usual for anything in its perfection phase. But, all in all, such tests provide a good direction of your stronger areas which you may or may not have been aware up until now. If nothing else, just try these out for fun.

2. Evaluate your Strengths and Weaknesses

Proper evaluation of your good and not so good traits is important not only for securing a nicer job or starting a business/profession but equally for living a well-informed life. Please be assured that there is nothing like a weakness or strength. An apparent strength for some situation, may be a weakness for some other, or vice versa. This general classification of strengths and weaknesses is best avoided for looking at practical results achieved by proper evaluations. Strengths and weaknesses touch every aspect of your existence and their deeper awareness help you in knowing yourself in right context and better perspective. Your individual qualities are too personal a matter and are a God gift to certain extent. It is your fundamental right to know about them in every possible clarity so that you can create your defenses against weaknesses or shortcomings and build upon your strengths or positivity.

No one is born with strengths, except for few typical forces associated with genetics. Most strengths stem from your interests and efforts. Interests always evolve on the basis of curiosity and willingness to learn. Curiosity makes you inquisitive about certain aspects of life and willingness to learn help you gain proficiency in those very aspects. Constant inquisitiveness encourages you to learn about them more through experience. In due course, as you put in more efforts and gain more experience, those aspects come out as your strengths. On the contrary, traits which fail to catch your curiosity also fail to fire your willingness to learn and practice, ultimately remain out of your reach and get branded as weaknesses. Once you get full clarity about this process, your perception for both strengths and weaknesses shall develop required neutrality. Please go through this process and re-examine your strengths and weaknesses all over afresh.

Evaluating your strengths and weaknesses can be incredibly intimidating, as there are lots of characteristics that may represent either. It is important that you are honest with yourselves about what you are good at, and what needs improvement. In the ultimate analysis of this exercise, you should be clear of traits that you are better blessed or have acquired with efforts, and vice versa, and use those findings every time you make a choice, small or big. If done dispassionately over long periods, this awareness turns invaluable because it helps you focus on the right things in an optimal manner. This tremendously improves your 'efforts to results' ratio, the usual input to output ratio. In Cricketing terms, this very ratio is called strike rate and clearly helps in understanding performance potential of each player. When you swim with the current, you can always expect your ratio/strike rate to be higher than when you swim against the currents. More than making you extra resourceful, this newfound awareness goes to improve your self-confidence and self-esteem and take you one step closure to know your authentic self as well.

3. Develop liking for Self

Self-love is a state of appreciation for oneself that grows from actions supporting physical, psychological and spiritual growth. Self-love is very dynamic and keep growing with every action taken in right direction. Every time you direct your actions towards your set goals or when you are able to operate within your boundaries or are able to withstand temptations, you take one baby step towards self-love. After all self-love is not about a makeover using makeup artist or putting designer dress for looking good, but a sense of being sufficient and likeable in terms of living desired life.

Yes, loving self is very important for living well as it even let us accept our deficiencies in positive manner. Speaking generally, we underestimate own strengths and other's weaknesses. But concept of loving self requires us to be more generous and not judge our self harsher. Being in love with our internal self only motivates us to be positive and do more. Let us not forget that our views about self immensely contribute towards our physical and psychological health. As already seen over and over again, the quest for understanding your real self requires living intentionally here and now. Love for self helps you in doing so. Let your life be based on clear sense and direction of purpose and design. Let every action you take gets guided towards that. Besides taking good care of your physical and psychological health, you must ensure that only right kind of people remain in your life.

This simple approach requires us to forget accumulated burden like tough childhood, below-average academic achievements, being bullied or abused, troubled relationship, failures to capitalize on opportunities gone by, inability to achieve much towards professional excellence, etc. How can you expect to find love for self if you are exhausted carrying above kind of load on your poor shoulders all the times? What is gone is gone, carrying burden of past did not help anyone ever, your fate is unlikely to be any different. Winners shake past events and build future on present while weak continue clinging with the past. You have a choice to make and decide which way to move. With consistent practice, you have to grow your muscle of self-love.

As per advice from experts, you need not focus on self-love, *per say*, but to focus on being someone loving. This means allowing love to flow through your system as often as possible. General suggestions explained in previous chapter, if dully practiced for some length of time, significantly contribute in augmenting flow love for self by making yourself all the more loveable. Look for love in everything you do, for example, focus on what you love about people, focus on things you appreciate, focus on subjects you love to discuss among friends, focus on what you love about your job or profession. Focusing over all such real-life scenarios help adjust your body for positive emotions and help augment your jest for life. You have to develop ability to break everything into small little pieces and find small beautiful aspects in all those pieces.

4. Don't Make Everything Personal

Yes, at times there are situations where others take offensive positions forcing a person to take things on personal level. But in general, others got no time to conspire against others all the times. Normal people do not enjoy hurting others, so it is useless to think that others are teaming to let you down. Few may end up doing it here and there but that is most likely out of ignorance and mostly without any ill will. Misunderstandings happen due to differences in perceptions. As such, continuously guarding against others eats up too much of your precious energy. In any case, what others say or do is reflection of their own reality and in no way deserve too much of attention. Taking things personally is a sure way of making a tiny moment into an unpleasant and uncomfortable episode. You stand to gain much more by diverting your energy towards productive use.

Suffering from some or the other insecurity, that end up making you feel trapped and taking the event personally, is also quite normal to expect. For example, for some people, dominating religious or cultural beliefs are considered uncompromisable and touching their sentiments in these areas is sufficient to blow their fuse. Please ensure you are not one of them. For the purpose of developing better understanding of Self, you must identify the triggers of events where you invariably tend to get personal. May be there are particular people who make your defenses go up. Low level of physical energy is yet another common trigger for getting into boxing corners far too quickly.

People are also strongly advised to monitor all their dominant emotions in action and dig out to find the real causes behind triggering their immediate explosions. Understanding all such triggers is essential to appreciate your reactions in transparent manner. Such comprehension about self alone facilitates process of self-healing against getting personal because right knowledge allows you to prepare in advance and takes away the very surprise that fuels the initial spark turning into full blaze. In due course of your journey, and with effect of other practices being discussed yielding result, you are likely to gain ability to avoid situations defusing the triggers much before the damage gets done or will allow you to ignore words and actions of other people as well as your own negative self-talks. You may need to regularly remind yourselves that there is no need to react to opinions of others. Feeling guilty or ashamed or feeling inferior to others in any way are all useless feelings that need to be kept under check. And it is possible as we do come across people who refuse to react even when very personal attacks and abuses get hurled upon them. We can never gain control over actions of others, but gaining power of modulating our own reactions to others looks entirely feasible.

5. Forget and Forgive

Vengeful behaviour has remained with human culture all through and weak as well as strong people have been using it alike from the very beginning. At time, there may also be genuine reasons to return blows of others in their own currency. We get hurt by words or actions from others, and in return we want them to experience hurt as well. On some occasions, such feelings get overwhelmed and take over our lives, disrupting relationships and going up to disrupting our ability to live normal life. As a result, our joy, zest for living, and drive to accomplish long term dreams, get compromised. Subconsciously, we may very well conclude logically that we need to hold a grudge to punish others but whose loss it leads to? Worst happens when holding such grudge for long becomes part of thoughts and behavior. Psychologically, your inability to forgive and let go comes from internal need to prove that your stance is absolutely correct. But this attitude of 'they are wrong, and I am right' is always extremely draining and life-consuming. There is no way to see what it does to others involved, but it always leaves you more miserable for sure.

Let us be selfish for a moment and ask a simple question to ourselves. Having grudges, hatred, envy or malice towards others helps whom? Does it help us in any way towards our achievements, happiness or fulfillment? No marks for guessing that not forgiving others only hurts us, and us alone. Forgiveness is a power and a virtue adorned only by the strongest. That is why you should behave like stronger person and forgive wrongs done by others to you as soon as possible. Carrying resentment, anger, sufferings and pain on your shoulders is like walking with dead weight. That is going to cost you time and energy and only promotes negativity. Forgiving, on the other hand, sets you free instantly. This is best tool for feeling light and charged.

At times you resort to using silence, anger, or withholding your love and support in order to convey resentment. You may be doing it to remain in control of situation. By refusing to forget and forgive, and digging your heels in with stubborn resentment instead, you are allowing the actions of another person to dictate your reactions and impact your emotions. When you are unable to forgive, you are bound to bog down with negativity; your anger creates obstacles that stand in your way preventing you from feeling and acting in the right manner. This way, you hold yourselves back, not the other person.

6. Experience challenges but make peace with failures

This persistent fear of failures keeps you holding back from aiming at bigger opportunities involving some element of associated risks. Taking aim on such opportunities may result either in failure or success. But not trying out surely ends all chances of success. And success removes chances for fear and failure. Taking shots on challenging opportunities helps you realize that fears are always not well founded. Any event of non-success is not a failure until such time that you accept it as a failure. Success in most initiatives is like trial and error. Failure also offers possibility of learning valuable lessons. If so, it is not fair to consider it as failure. People gaining wisdom by this trial and error are indeed winners. Most successful people stepped up their efforts without getting demoralized from their initial failures and errors. Do not stop trying again and again. Let us also look at mistakes vs failures. Mistakes are nothing but wrong selection of technique to succeed. Perseverance is the key as bad results do not demoralize people with perseverance.

Failure is always an uncomfortable experience and nobody wants to go through frequent failures. Because, we are taught from a young age that failure is bad, we begin to fear any misstep or work on an idea that might result in failure. Over time, we start finding it easier to just play it safe. This attitude stops us from taking big risks or pursue crazy ideas. After all, no one wants to be seen as "deficient" or ''failure" by others. On the hand, not taking risks also inhibit your chances of reaping bigger dividends. Playing it safe all the time is a sure way to lead a life of a mediocre. Many people remain stuck in a job they hate instead of doing something they really love. There are people who ignore their talents and instead pursue occupations that are not too challenging. That is how most of us make it difficult to reach to full potential. In short, we end up living a life that pales in comparison to the life we could be living only if we were not having the fear of failing.

We all know that Edison, the inventor of bulb, failed very many times but he did not give up and kept trying newer ways until success was forced to come his way. What did Edison say about failing? When a reporter asked, "How did it feel to fail 1,000 times?" Edison replied, "I didn't fail 1,000 times. The light bulb was an invention with 1,000 steps." He considered every failure nothing more than yet another step on the way. "Great success is built on failure, frustration, even catastrophe." Albert Einstein did not speak until he was four years-old and did not read until he was seven. People say that you just don't know the real taste of success unless you have failed couple of times. One can pick up a list of highly success people from various fields in recent time including but not limited to Abraham Lincoln, Winston Churchill, Charles Darwin, Henry Ford, Steve Jobs, and many more, the most common thread connecting all these luminaries is the fact that all of them went through several failures in their early life.

And why go so far as Indian super achievers in multiple fields like Rajnikanth, Dhirubhai Ambani, MS Dhoni, Dr. Abdul Kalam, Narayana Murthy, Amitabh Bachchan and Gautam Adani, few big names from our immediate memory do share same story of facing innumerable adversities during their early days, many of which would have been judged as classical failures. For example, first company formed by Mr. Murthy, before Infosys, tanked within a year and half or as late as the year 2000, Mr. Bachchan had no films, no money, host of legal cases and tax authorities putting notice on his house for recovering tax dues. But their ultimate achievements are here for everyone to see and get inspired.

Any attempt to look at failure as an error is wrong. Mistakes or failures are made by people who experiment. Safest way of not making a mistake is to do nothing. More you challenge yourself, more likely you get exposed to chances of failure. Failure can be bad, indifferent or good depending on the learning made out of it. No one wins playing blame games. Failures provide you wisdom so long as you learn from them. Accept that being defensive all the times is too dull and boring.

Failures are also important because these help in identifying the real friends/ supporters because good times are always accompanied by the crowd but the ones who stand with you during your harsh times are your true friends. Besides, getting pushed to the wall by failures always develop respect for success. Also, success after failures taste much better than success without failures. Failures should be taken as a part of life and let it make you a better and stronger person. The journey to success is never easy. Real failure is when you fail to get up, and look failure in the eye. So, never stop trying because that is what leads you to success.

How this discussion about failures is relevant for understanding self? Simply because sum of failures and success have direct and everlasting impact on our self-confidence, self-esteem as well as spiritual self. You cannot find your core unless you have experienced real life from one extreme to another. What all you could do after failures, cannot be anticipated without going through actual process of failure. Repetitive failures alone let you know if you have challenged yourself completely or not.

7. See through impermanence of the visible

Looks, money, position, influence or possessions are all very subjective and matter differently to different people. Even if there is someone who seems to have more than you, how relevant is that? Impermanence allows people to cope more easily with trying times. Once you arrive at conclusion that life is indeed transient, you also develop acceptance that everything in life (your spouse, children, parents, friends, health, status, titles and bank balance included) is also not permanent. This understanding, in turn, let you respond with grace every time anything perceived critical or valuable goes away or is taken back from you.

Accepting fact about impermanence brings a unique mental calmness and balance. As per modern psychology that balanced perspective results in cultivating positive well-being, besides eliminating negative mental states. This concept happens to be a foundational Buddhist concept. Each one of us has the capacity to enjoy living life completely but only if we remain fully conscious of the fact that negative happenings are always possible and can't be avoided at all times. Let us never forget that everything comes with a expiry date.

> *"Awareness of impermanence and appreciation of our human potential will give us a sense of urgency that we must use every precious moment."* — Dalai Lama

8. Examine your Priorities

You are unique and you alone know yourself. Please try to be original in your thinking by forgetting all about others around or your own past situation. It is quite possible to develop habit of thinking in a spontaneous and random manner. To be creative and effective, allow your thinking to be unorganized (which incidentally is totally different than disorganized). Practice thinking in a free flowing manner going from one subject to another. That is how you expect to see new solutions with alternate perspective. Thinking beyond the obvious requires training your brain to break through its normal tendency to jump to premature conclusions by just glancing on the obvious which may sound reasonable on the surface but may prove completely incorrect assumption. This premature arrival on conclusions is the sign of a lazy mind not willing to look beyond the obvious.

Thinking is far more important than what we normally believe. Content and quality of what we think in our day-to-day life, speaks a lot about who we are or have potential to become. Our thoughts lead to our actions and that is how destinies get made over time. A good comparison of your priorities with other people you look up to, tells a lot about you as well. Of course, not most of us actually maintain very detailed list of priorities but we must remain open to the idea even when we believe to have our priorities in the best order. Let us give our self a shock and assume for a moment that our house is burning down.

Now, what all would you like to salvage? It's amazing how a fictitious idea of house being on fire got the power to expose presence or absence of major priorities in your life. One may be sentimental to save gift items received or he may be practical to save money, ornaments and tax records while another person may have yet another logic to decide something else. There may also be other situations helping us identify our priorities, and all those situations are equally good. For example, our actions in the face of peer criticism and possible ostracization can reveal our priorities. During the process of setting priorities for life, you gain clarity about your goals in their relative importance. Knowing things that are important to you boost your confidence which gets reflected in your actions.

Priorities are about choosing what is most important to you at a given point in time. Your resources in terms of money, time and energy are always limited and scarce. Setting priorities is about how we allocate our limited resources. Thus, priorities work like a bridge between our requirements and resources. When we are clear about our individual purpose, then we understand how to dedicate our limited resources. Today, the world presents to us numerous choices and alternatives that are alluring to our senses but are not necessarily beneficial and thus, may lead us to a path of wasting our productive years in life. We must have the wisdom and discipline to make the right choices about most important things of our lives.

9. Monitor yourself while experiencing strong feelings

At times, we come across strong feelings and get over angry, sad, happy, or excited. Understanding what sets off these stronger-than-normal reactions, identifying their root cause, does help in improving own understanding about Self. For example, you are at a theater watching some serious movie and get angry about people talking during a movie. Now, the source of that anger may be disruption of your attention, desire to show others how powerful you are, violation of common etiquettes, disruption of public order or a feeling of disrespect. Each of these triggers require solutions which significantly vary from each other. Right solution will come only after knowing the exact trigger. Similarly, there are always multiple reasons for all strong reactions and going deeper for each of them, in a systematic manner, is worth the investment of attention in the underlying exercise of monitoring the real triggers.

Besides obvious causes, there may be igniting causes rooted in other issues. You have to explore even deeper to identify and pin point those. That is why this exercise need to be conducted for longer periods. Watch out for repression and transference. Repression is when you don't want to think about something, so you force yourself to forget it even when something adverse happens. Transference is when you emotionally react to one thing, while the underlying trigger lies somewhere else. Both these behaviors, although common in nature, are unhealthy. It is imperative to spot the reality before developing right understanding about your core. Else, you run the risk of getting misguided resulting in poor results.

Perfecting the simple art of taking a brief pause is considered important in this respect as well. You must train yourself to take a small pause every time you are tempted to speak or act under influence of your feelings. Eventually, this habit travels through entire thinking process. You cannot imagine how a split-second delay can make a world of emotional difference in terms of calming you down and saving you from taking undesired actions or reactions.

Please don't take these simple ideas lightly as it might take very long conscious efforts to develop desired expertise, especially when it comes to applying it under emotionally charged situations. This lethal weapon is best used just before you are about to lose temper. At that moment, your anger is boiling hot, and your fuse is about to go off. People are known to suffer heavy impacts for wrongly losing their temper, including ruining career or damaging relationships. To remind yourselves to take a moment to reflect on your emotions, to breathe, and to responsibly respond in that charged environment, is certainly challenging but doable. You can surely look around and find people within your surroundings doing as advised above, why not you?

10. Be Willing to See Change in Unchangeable

Normally we come across suggestions that we must begin with the belief that massive changes in life are possible. But for people regularly failing in making even small changes in life, such suggestions come out as theoretical and/or impractical sermons. It is normal that a person whose new year resolutions do not even last over days, does not get motivated to suddenly believe in these as gospel truths. This is precise reason to advocate "being willing" as the very first and formidable lane to be taken to enter the expressway of transforming life. But a complete skeptic may never even try to enter the toll gate of that expressway even when he knows that his destination can be reached faster using the toll road. The journey of such a skeptic converting into an unconditional believer is no less than adopting a new religion.

The only window connecting these two extremes is 'being willing' to try something new, something afresh, to give another try to succeed. But the attitude of being willing must come with eagerness as well as readiness to give sincere try for things to fructify. And let us remember that being willing is much more than wanting something. You have to be ready without any persuasion or force or greed. Being willing does not focus on wins alone as it remains open for embracing failure as well. It is quite possible that you may have loved it and lost in the past. Being willing opens door for newer attempts.

The positive trait of 'Being Willing', either acquired or cultivated, holds immense opportunities waiting to be unfolded. Do not restrict yourself from diving deep into this powerful exploration and do it ever so willingly. It might work or not work; the point is whether you are willing to give a try or not.

11. Take Notice of how and why you interact with others

When you interact with people, there are specific ways that you connect with each of them. You look forward to greet some, wait to be greeted by some other or just wish to ignore someone's presence. And there are others whom you just wish to put down. These different preferences are a result of your subconscious level biases. May be, you choose to spend time with people that have more money than you. May be, you feel shy in presence of people from opposite gender. Also, may be, you love company of people who need guidance on career choice. Some of you may be willing to engage in discussions with even strangers on current affairs of the world. Some other people do everything to avoid company of people who draw everyone's attention because they are categorized as funny or spontaneous. All such situations seem very natural and you may have been ignorant about your preferences or may not have given much attention to the fact that you indeed have defined preferences for different people while interacting socially.

Observing such behaviors repeatedly certainly teach you things about yourself and help you know what is important to you, and what is not. For example, when you choose to spend time with richer friends, it shows that you want to feel wealthier by letting yourself pretend you are equal to your friends. Feeling shy in presence of opposite sex, similarly, indicate your orthodox upbringing, being over-conscious for opposite sex, about your morality conflict or it might even be indication of you suffering from inferiority complex. You alone can evaluate each possible cause and refine your understanding by repetitive observations. Again, pin pointing right reasons alone will facilitate getting over them.

Similarly, you should pay attention to what you actually listen and retain from talks with people vs what you tell them about. There are always only few key points that remain with you out of long discussions with people. What you retain, what you pass over, what you emphasize, what you feel elated about, what you feel offended with, what you wish to repeat again and what you regret saying, are all live issues that go to reveal a lot about your own personality. The gaps, if any, indicate about your issues needing attention. You also need to learn from your interactions with your close friends and family. There might be issues relating to things lost in translation where you may be reading their words wrongly. Both verbal and non-verbal communications with people around are good sources for you to know yourself with clarity and conviction.

You are due for multiple surprises about many aspects of your set likes and dislikes being played repetitively during all your communications without you being even aware about them. Once this exercise gets completed and you begin your future communications with expanded awareness of all these aspects, what do you think happens to your communication quality? For sure, you will be sweetly surprised having substantive and effective communication.

12. See how long you can wait for gratification

Studies have shown that people who are able to delay gratification, generally get through life smoothly. Such students get better grades and study up to higher levels while such adults maintain a healthier body and achieve better success in their respective professions. Recollect about situations where you had opportunity to engage in gratifications and revisit actions you took in those situations. Did you go for enjoyment, were you apprehensive but still caved in for temptations or you were able to significantly delay or avoid altogether the gratification and come out unscathed? Make a self-evaluation, and if you conclude having trouble in delaying gratification, there is a project waiting for you. This is something important and having wider repercussions to look out for and work on to ensure success in life. Stanford did a famous experiment about this concept and called the same as the Marshmallow Experiment, where they watched how some kids reacted when presented with marshmallow treats and then followed their progress through life, over the course of many decades. No wonder, the children who put off their treat in favor of a bigger reward did better in school, work, and health-related areas.

Instant gratification is a habit where we cave in to avoid short-term discomforts, and instead, indulge in fleeting pleasures that ultimately result in long term pains. In other words, we invent excuses not to do something because of the pain it creates in the immediate moment even when we remain fully aware that such action has associated costs over longer periods. Instant gratification often appears as harmless procrastination but, in reality, it is clearly a form of self-sabotage where we knowingly get caught up by temporal temptations offered by life sacrificing much more meaningful long-term bigger benefits. Yes, agreed that pleasures of the moment may seem very enticing and seductive but bearing small temporary pain may be worth multiplied gains in the long-term. Why should anyone ignore to invest all his money on such an investment proposal? It is in this background that Indian thoughts always warned human against pleasures at all levels and at all times.

Indulging in instant gratification is a clear-cut sign of lack of self-discipline. It is a minor irritant capable of snowballing into a gigantic obstacle in due course. A sure indicator of our poor control over emotional and carnal urges, this subsequently results into significant consequences impacting many other live issues of life. It does not matter if you were caving in public space under gaze of others or in absolute privacy of your exclusive personal space away from every living soul. Surrendering to temptations remains poor indicator with adverse impacts without exception. You have no choice but to invent your own delay-devices, test them and fix them in your system to gain freedom from temptations and playing around short-term convenience and comforts. Anyone attempting to reach to his authentic self has to develop the capability of ignoring instant gratification at all costs and at all times, without exception.

13. Analyze yourself when you get 'to tell' or 'be told'

As human we certainly love our independence and it is natural to crave for autonomy or seeking control of every situation in life. Who does not aspire to be an Alfa male who takes charge, imposes his will on others and not the other way round? We all wish to intimidate our surrounding, be unquestioned in-charge, no matter what is the situation, even when we run the risk of getting branded as loud or brash. We want to be our own boss and hate if others make rules for us. But let us not forget that everyone is a rebel in the making. Also, it is but natural to question the authority-in-charge and feel good to do the opposite of what we are asked to do. But people do widely differ in terms of degree of opposition. Some merely feel uncomfortable, others feel strongly annoyed, some other just panic and few others may feel deeply angry. These reactions indeed represent different shades of opposition to a similar intensity of diktats. This degree of defiance exhibits individual level of psychological reluctance and is worth taking notice of.

You better look at your own level of reluctance and take inventory of your reactions to such situations on different occasions. You have to observe and analyze your reactions and conclude how much poking you require before getting provoked. Remember that there is nothing wrong with needing someone to give you instructions and guidance before doing a task. It is just something to be aware of so that you can better understand and control your own behavior when important things come up.

Similarly, when it is your turn to leave instructions about others, you need to look at your thought process. Someone may be a bossy, a guide, a coach, an elder, a teacher, a captain, or a commander. Each type speaks about different styles having different repercussions. Besides the style, you need to check about your sensitivities of your interaction with others, especially when you are in charge. Do you behave in same manner at all times and with all people or you act selectively? Each of these responses say different things about you. Depending on the situation, you may be required to re-train your mind and manage your attitude to be more disciplined and accommodating. After all, you will like your inner rebel to fuel your growth and not bring you down. You may like to develop sense of balance where everything is best weighed in to see what is best for you and those around you. And ability to do right things even when things are inconvenient, differentiate the winners from the rest.

14. Take Notice of the way you react in times of personal crisis or tough situations

There are unique parts of a person's character that find expressions only in crisis times. Situations like loss of loved ones, involvement in major accident, break-up in romantic relationship, heated arguments with a close family member or relative, failure of business, coming to know of major illness or loss of employment, do not happen every day but got capacity to change destiny of people involved and those impacted directly or even indirectly. How one reacts under such situations, speaks a lot about his hidden or restrained parts of character.

There is a saying "when the going gets tough, the tough get going." It is a different story that most of the times tough going overwhelms people and bring them to their knees. Recollection about how you reacted while tension got sky high and analyze how you wish you could have reacted, teaches you some important lessons about your ability to withstand crisis. But this point applies only for a person who has gone over any such scenario in real life because just imagining it can only generate hypothetical responses which may be clouded by bias and not be accurate as to how the person would really react.

But there are other general scenarios which can very well be imagined for effective learning. Let us say you get forced to relocate to a new city for setting up new profession or transfer of job. Imagining just one such move may bring out many indications about your personality. There can be many things that you can go over in context of such imaginary scenario. For example, what kind of friends you would like to make at the new place, what kind of house you would like to choose to live in, what kind of lifestyle you would like to start, which all membership would you like to pay for, what kind of neighbors would you like to begin socializing with, what kind of sports/performing arts you would like to work on and so on. Honest answers to such scenarios may help you becoming aware of your real-life preferences as well as reveal you your priorities and what you are looking for in your social interactions.

15. Analyze your behavior while sitting in position of power

To begin with, let us settle the real meaning and context of being in position of power. Psychological research has redefined power as one's capacity to alter another person's condition or state of mind by managing resources or punishments. This definition emphasizes individual's capacity to affect others and not his actual acts. This definition applies across relationships, contexts, and cultures. You can be in position of power without actually trying to control, coerce, or dominate someone. So, power is not something limited to power-hungry individuals or organizations alone; it is part of every social interaction where people have the capacity to influence one another's states, which is really every moment of life. It helps us understand how children wield power over their parents, and spouses exercise power over each other. So power is not something we should avoid, nor it necessarily involves actual act of domination or submission.

When in position of power, you must look at the effect it has on your behavior. As a standard template, people with power tend to become harsher, less open to receive suggestions, less willing to know subjects in detail, casual in forming opinions, more controlling, and overtly suspicious. But this stereotype does not apply to everyone. So, analyzing your behavior when in power speaks a lot about your inner core. When you find yourself making decisions that affect others, think about why you are really making that choice, or even more importantly, why did you not opt for the alternatives available. Was it the right thing to do or did it made you feel being in control? The power paradox requires that you be ever vigilant against the corruptive influences of power and its ability to distort the way you see yourselves and treat others.

16. Let go of your Defensiveness

To be defensive is to react with over protective mentality which is not proportionate to the requirement of the situation. It is an impulsive and reactive way of responding. Where one should have listened with open mind, defensiveness forces him to defend his position yielding metaphorical weapons as shields. You tend to become defensive either to seek protection against feeling of hurts or shame. Basically, defensive behavior is to play the blame game and shift attention to the faults of person in front. In the process, you start feeling better about your own self.

Defensive attitude involves strong psychological factors preventing us from accepting unlikable truth about ourself. Now, it might help you feel better in the short run but ultimately, it is going to haunt you back. Unfortunately, picking up signs of being defensive are very difficult because they come from within. But if you look carefully, there are instances where it stops you from listening to what the person in front is telling, or you resorting to making excuses every time you get blamed for something. Counter blaming the blamer or accusing the accuser, are also clear indications of your defensiveness at work. Allowing such a behavior has many negative impacts on the relationships you have with others around.

Holding on to things from past, and that too negative in character, is another common reason of being defensive. But clinging on to pains does not fix anything. People justify holding on unpleasant emotions from past because they wish those feelings to remain integral part of their identity. In some cases, people make their pains as essence of their entire existence. Replaying the past over and over again does not change it. You may wish that things were different but that also does not make any difference. When it comes to the hurts and pains from the past, all you can do is accept and let it go. That is the only way real changes have chance to convert into reality. We must allow things to go, even when it feels almost impossible. Deciding to hold on to the past only holds us back from creating a strong sense of self. Our self should never be defined by past but what we are in the present and what potential we have to become in future.

You will be naturally defensive about admitting these kind of things to yourself, but if you wish to understand how it works, then you have to go over your defensiveness. Even if you do not let those barriers down for other people, you have to do it for yourself. Becoming less defensive about your weaknesses can also mean opening yourself up to getting help from other people and making amends. If you are more open to discussion, criticism, and change, then other people can really help you understand and improve yourself.

17. Be Honest with Yourself

Haven't we learned about honesty being the best policy from very early childhood itself? But did we really made efforts to practice it in real life as well, may be no. Somehow, the simple rule of "fake it till you make it" has almost become a social norm in modern times. Actually, we lie to ourselves a lot more than we would like to believe. On all those occasions our intelligent mind comes up with weird rationale justifying why we resorted to lies. But making self believe that questionable choices were made for noble or logical reasons, where you were actually vindictive or lazy, is of no use.

Hiding reality of our faults does not make us a better person. Let us be open minded and honest to see the faults where they lie. Agreed, you have to cross over your hardwired coding of blaming others for everything wrong happening around. Be honest and call spade a spade. Be a man and take responsibility of your flaws as well. Discovering less likeable truths about ourself need fixing and not justification. Let us take such issues as opportunity to take those problems head on instead of just pretending like they do not exist. Being honest with yourself always makes life easier, remove bunch of complications and makes life a lot more beautiful, or less ugly in the least. Being honest brings down your dependence on others and helps in developing self-love irrespective your deficiencies or flaws. That self-love, in return, is always regarded as a beginning of being contended and internally peaceful.

For understanding own self better, we have no choice but to be courageous enough to being initially vulnerable. Sooner than later, you have to walk over your old wounds. So, be ready to face your fears head on, as early as possible. Developing habit of self-talks on regular basis and by living in solitude goes a long way in weighing right options. People also suggest maintaining a daily diary where questions like "what did I do right today and what can I do better tomorrow" helps. It is said that it is much harder to lie to our self when we wish to write down our thoughts. Learning how to be honest with yourself is not just about reflecting on your past, it also covers dreaming about ideal future as well.

18. Give attention to words spoken by others

Other people you interact with are generally of three types. There are people who do not care about you, some of them want you down and under but there are also a tiny minority who really care about you and will be happy to see you succeed. But listening to what all these three types of people say about you is a good idea at all times. Each of them may say things that may be less likable but more informative or revealing about your own self. Sometimes, we do wrong things and there are people who try to warn us against our behavior. But it matters only if you listen in the first place. Quoting Dr. Suess, the American Author, "be who you are and say what you feel, because those who mind don't matter, and those who matter don't mind".

On the other hand, people of wisdom have suggested to necessarily keep some of your critics in your inner circle because you can always be sure of their finding faults in whatever you do. There is a famous sermon by Sant Kabir where he says:

> *"Nindak niyare rakhiye aangan kuti chhawaye,*
> *Bin sabun pani bina nirmal karat subhav"*

which translate as "always keep your critics in your close proximity where they can watch you closely, because they will let you keep your attitude spotless without requiring soap or water". This goes to prove that receiving feedback from your critics, and acting on it for your own sake, is not even a modern-day idea. This is a proven way of knowing about your missteps, allowing you to go for course correction without losing time.

At times, it can be difficult to ignore someone who upsets you or causes you grief. This can be even more difficult when that individual is someone you have to see or interact with on a regular basis. But often what they say should be taken as good as it let you see area of possible improvements. Outsider's analysis of how you behave always provides you meaningful inputs. Think about what people have said in the past and ask for their new opinions about your behavior. For example, your friend might notice that you tend to exaggerate. May be that it is unintentional on your part and happens just in the flow. This feedback may help you to know that your perception of reality is a bit off. There is a big difference between evaluating what they say about you and letting that opinion control your life and actions. You should not tailor your behavior to suit other people unless it is highly essential. Make changes only if you also agree with them, and because you also see positive outcomes out of them and not because someone else tells you that you should.

> *"That's been one of my mantras – focus and simplicity. Simple can be harder than complex: You have to work hard to get your thinking clean to make it simple. But it's worth it in the end because once you get there, you can move mountains."*
>
> — Steve Jobs

19. Give advice as often as possible

For long time, taking advice from others has been advocated as a beneficial practice for improving self. But recent time scientific studies prove otherwise. Now it is well established that giving advice helps the person giving it as much as it helps those receiving it. There are clear evidence suggesting that giving advice motivates achievement by raising confidence of the provider as it escalates his intuitive sense. The findings showed people struggling with goal achievement getting benefited more from giving advice than receiving it. Giving advice implies the giver possesses, as opposed to lacks, the skill in question. Receiving advice, inadvertently, implies the opposite.

Giving advice will often give you a great opportunity to think through your own problems and reevaluate them from new angles. When looking at someone else's situation, you are likely to think in more neutral way, which generally is not the case for your own situations. You do not even have to do this activity for real as a simple scenario building also helps in some ways. But if you are actually able to help others, it is even better as helping your friends, family, and even strangers, in any case, is a nice thing to do. By thinking through your past experiences and what is really important to you for the future, you end up refining your own understanding about yourself.

20. Letting go of Expectations

It might sound harsh but truth remains that most societies throughout the world live and breathe over-expectations at every moment. Parents have high expectations from children, employees have from employers, friends from each other, elders from younger generation, public from governments and haves' nots from those have it. Interestingly, intimate relationships top the list of over expectations from each other. But think for a moment. Is it fair to expect some other person to be who we want them to be? All expectations are basically arbitrary. Others are what they are and we should leave it on them if, when and how they wish to change things around them. It is indeed time to put aside all sorts of expectations from one and all. You are captain of your own ship and so is everyone else. Not expecting anything from others, as well from own self, is panacea, a sure cure for a great deal of anxiety, stress, disappointments, frustration, anger, depression and host of other negative emotions we experience in life.

> *"Blessed is he who expects nothing, for he shall never be disappointed."*
>
> — Alexander Pope

Expectations are product of imaginations. And imaginations are unreal and tend to go wrong all the time. Imaginations always get built on host of assumptions and probable scenarios. The entire process of building expectations of all types involves a number of ifs and buts. That is why outcome of predictions can go in one way or the other. So, when expectations are built over wrong presumptions, why should you go through the disappointments and resentments of their not coming true? Yes, we all are wired to want things happening the way we like them but we are better advised to let go of such expectations and settle for what life is actually like. The moment you let go expectations, you will be more open to seeing what new experiences might make you happy and fulfilled. Life is a crazy roller-coaster and you are going to encounter a lot of things that scare you because they are new or different but do not close yourself to those experiences. They might make you happier than you have ever been.

....

As already mentioned, some of these tips may not be found directly relating to our subject under discussions but each of these contribute, bit by bit, in uncovering many layers of wrong impressions, making us conscious for which we may have been acting unconsciously until now or inviting us to start doing many other things that are capable of bringing our self into close contact of our deeper personality. After achieving good progress on above mentioned practices, we ought to become familiar with our reality and our ignorance get exposed. Continuing the recommended practices over longer periods, our internal content is expected to come out in open with naked clarity. Going forward on our journey of understanding of our real self, stark realities of our negative impulses like greed, desires, attachments, immorality, unethical behavior, aggression, lust, envy, etc. start spilling out opening the pandora's box of our unwanted but living reality. Reality bites hard and for many people, this brings shock of their life forcing them to even resort to extreme steps.

In the ultimate analysis, each of these tips contribute rather directly in developing more intimate relationship with our own self. Perfection gained on these suggestions and tips, however, shall go a long way in preparing the matured explorer in his ultimate quest for diving to the deepest part of his inside called by different names.

In the following section, the reader will be exposed to Ancient Indian take of this important aspect of Self besides touching its philosophical and spiritual connect.

5

Self and Ancient Indian Philosophical Views

Ancient Indian philosophical views provide a well-structured and conceptually comprehensive take on Self like none other culture anywhere in the whole world. The very concept of self rests on a combination of gross entity of body and mind and subtle qualities of intellect, discrimination and wisdom. Simplest expression of self is the sense of the notion of "I am". Thus "I am" becomes another aspect after body/mind and intellect. In Indian contexts, this aspect largely revolves around inward looking quest. Such a quest has been explained in dozens of Upanishads and can be summarized by saying that ultimate truth of everything in this universe lies inside the human being itself.

Teachings of those Upanishads bring out the fact that it is only by diving deep within that we can find Supreme Reality and a person who masters that becomes man of wisdom in his own capacity. In modern parlance, we can say that teachings from Upanishads highlight existence of a 'superman' residing inside each of us waiting to be found and acknowledged. But that finding and communication becomes possible only after gaining required wisdom through study, assimilation of scriptures and self-contemplation. In short, Indian wisdom is based upon subjective and qualitative experiences which, incidentally, is diagonally opposite to the Western view on knowledge focused on objective and quantitative aspects. But off late, Indian thoughts, evolved over last 5000 years of recorded history, are finally getting acknowledged even by modern time psychology thinkers who have started exploring man's awareness to fill the gap between his knowledge of inner world and that of the outer world.

As per one of the Indian thoughts, each person is his own creator, preserver and destroyer and it is not that difficult to comprehend why. Basically, we think therefore we exist. And since we exist, we keep thinking and desiring. This endless process ensures our continuity in the form of becoming and being, two significant states from which we are rarely free. We exist as individual identity arising from our thinking, our desires and attachments. That is how basically we are our own world. Authors of Upanishads believed normal people to be persistent, conscious of their identity, keen on self-examination and striving for self-improvements. In general, ancient sages conceived human being as subject of reasoning and actions and being responsible in moral and ethical spheres as well in their dealings with other people. The revered Ancient India principle of Karma is also said to impact a person's core and in perpetuity. Once again, this emphasis on inward focus of self stands apart Western thinking where external phenomena remain the center of attention.

For the sake of simplicity, let us look at two aspects of Self under discussion called as lower self and higher self. Lower self refers to undeveloped self that remains engaged in activities relating to survival and feel-good factors like eating, sleeping, procreating, enjoying luxuries. Upanishads call this self as the empirical self, the existential self. One which is subject to usual sorrows and sufferings of all kinds, physical and intellectual. This empirical self in unstable and is subject to change at all times. On the other hand, the higher self refers to the basic premise described as eternal, omnipotent, conscious, and intelligent being, who is one's real self. The true self or the Higher Self or unchanging Self, called Atman, that observes the empirical phenomena, is said to be unaffected and undying.

Incidentally, Westerner wisdom consider mind as a subject and part of transcendental entity or principle linked to soul. In other words, the mind and soul are perceived as one and the same in the West. But Vedanta scholars from India do not consider mind like that. Indian philosophies always considered mind as a gross entity emanating from and controlled by subtler entities, where subtler of all is Atman. According to the Advaita Vedanta, the true spiritual aspirant must eventually become intimately familiar with the workings of his internal sub-systems, his 'inner equipment'. He must listen to internal voice, then rigorously contemplate upon it, and finally, use the equipment (mind) to overcome the very equipment through meditation.

The concept of Self propagated by Upanishads can also be divided into three distinct categories – physical or material self, the relational self and finally the reflective or contemplative self, where the third aspect is considered as higher self or purer self. The difference between lower and higher self is planned to be taken in much detail at a later stage. But until such time, it is sufficient to know that the subject matter of our discussions as well as the self explained by Indian philosophies refers to only Higher Self. All later thoughts under Hinduism continue to consider Atman as distinct from individual personality, which include all normal habits, prejudices, desires, impulses, delusions, behaviors, pleasures, sufferings and fears. Human personality and Ahamkara shift, evolve or change with time, state the schools of Hinduism, but Atman does not. Considering its overriding importance, a detailed understanding of Atman will prove very helpful.

As per Wikipedia page on the same subject, "*The Higher Self is generally regarded as a form of being only to be recognized in a union with a divine source. In recent years the New Age faith has encouraged the idea of the Higher Self in contemporary culture, though the notion of the Higher Self has been interpreted throughout numerous historical spiritual faiths. Some denominations believe that the higher self is a part of an individual's metaphysical identity, while others teach that the higher self is essentially our tie to the heavens. Similar to the notion of the soul, the higher self can be defined by many different sects, while also being a topic of interest in the scientific and philosophical fields.*"

Atman of sages of Upanishads can also be loosely understood as spirit or soul. Incidentally, Atman is very first doctrine of Vedanta school of Hinduism and is considered as the inner most essence of an individual, the 'true self' or 'real self' of an individual which is beyond physical identity; which is internal, imperishable and beyond time unlike body, mind or even consciousness. Liberation from the cycle of life and death, the Samsara, is called Moksha and is taken as the ultimate aim for every living individual. Achieving Moksha is said to become possible after acquiring full self-knowledge, the Atma Gyan. Moksha is also called as Self-Realization of one's true self (Jivatma) where Brahman is considered as the Ultimate Reality.

All the six orthodox schools of Indian Philosophy, namely, Nyaya, Vaisesika, Samkhya, Yoga, Mimamsa, and Vedanta are based on the belief that there exist a 'Jiva' or 'Atman' in every living being. With literal meaning being 'that which breathes', Jiva is originally referred to the biological aspect of man's nature which goes on throughout life and consist of material body, principle of breath regulating the unconscious activities, and the principle of conscious activities (manas) which uses five sensory organs and five action organs. All these are organised by buddhi, the principle of intellect. Jainism too accepts this premise with its own interpretations. However, in total contrast of this, Buddhism and Charvak deny anything called Atman.

The Vedanta schools of Hinduism, however, differ about explanations of the relation between Brahman and Atman. While Shankaracharya of Advaita school believes Brahman and Atman to be identical, as per Ramanuja of Vishishtadvaita, the individual self is eternally one with and also different from the Brahman, the Universal self. In contrast of both these stands, Madhava of Dvaita school, holds that Jiva is eternally different from Brahman. But on the whole, Jiva the soul, is said to represent an idea of the divine mind and different souls are taken as members of the Supreme. The idea of perfection of soul is derived from Divine Creator alone.

Let us look at well quoted citation from Brihadaranyaka Upanishad 4.4.5 to get a real feel of the description summarized so far -

> *"That Atman is indeed Brahman. It is also identified with the intellect, the mind, and the vital breath, with the eyes and ears, with earth, water, air, and sky, with fire and with what is other than fire, with desire and the absence of desire, with anger and the absence of anger, with righteousness and unrighteousness, with everything — it is identified, as is well known, with what is perceived and with what is inferred. As Atman does and acts, so it becomes: by doing good it becomes good, and by doing evil it becomes evil. It becomes virtuous through good acts, and vicious through evil acts. Others, however, say, "The self is identified with desire alone. What it desires, so it resolves; what it resolves, so is its deed; and what deed it does, so it reaps."*

Similarly, Katha Upanishad, in Book 1, hymns 3.3 to 3.4, describes the widely cited analogy of chariot for the relation of "Soul, Self" to body, mind and senses. One of the translations of this hymn goes as:

> *"Know the Self as the rider in a chariot, and the body as simply the chariot. Know the intellect as the charioteer, and the mind as the reins. The senses, they say are the horses, and sense objects are the paths around them".*

There is yet another famous story in Mundaka Upanishad (3.1.1–2.) about two birds living in the same tree. The simple story proves very relevant for understanding the take on self, its challenges and final way out to evolve and merge Higher Self with

Supreme Self. It briefly lay out the entire path set for our spiritual journey, its goals and the challenges that we must be ready to face along the way. The story goes like:

> *"Two birds, bound together in close friendship, live in a tree. One lives amongst the lower branches while the other, a dazzling golden bird, perches high up at the very top of the tree. The lower bird keeps busy all day long relishing fruits of the tree picked by hopping from branch to branch. While looking for the sweet fruits, it ends up tasting many sour ones as well. The higher bird has no interest in eating any of the fruits of the tree and sits silently just peacefully observing the movements of lower bird. One day, the lower bird eats a particularly bitter fruit, is put off and gets totally tired of chasing after sweet fruits. Then it also decides to reach the higher bird, staying focused and carefully avoiding the temptations of fruits along the way. Soon the lower bird also begins to take on the qualities of the brilliant higher bird. Finally, the lower bird merges to become the higher bird. Soon after reaching to the top, it realizes that it was never separate from the higher bird as lower bird was just an illusion, like a dream that fades away upon waking up."*

The symbolic meaning of lower and higher birds in this story represents the ego and the higher Self respectively. As in the case of the two birds, the ego, the false "I" and the Self, the real "I" have an eternal brotherhood. They live together in the same body, no matter which body they take on. The tree represents the physical body. Ego is in essence the peaceful higher Self but it has forgotten its true nature and takes itself to be insecure and limited. It seeks to regain its inherent fullness in the only way it knows through the enjoyment of favorable things, people and situations in the outer world. The fruits of the tree represent the fruits of our karma, where good deeds accumulating good karma making us happy through enjoyable experiences. Our not-so-good past actions, on the other hand, reap bad karma and always bring us suffering and misery.

The Higher Self also lives in the same body, but it doesn't enjoy or suffer because it has no interest in gaining any worldly joys. It is merely a witness, abiding in its full, peaceful nature. Finally, when we have had enough of the fruitless search for enduring happiness in the world, we are sure to turn inwards with determination and sincere commitment. This is when we arrive at the threshold of spirituality. When we pursue spirituality with genuine sincerity, our egocentric desires and personality starts to crumble. We gain a greater inner poise and serenity as the beauty of the Self starts to shine through. Finally, we rediscover our true spiritual nature and realize our oneness with it.

Reaching for the True Self or Higher Self or Atman, called by some such names, is the very central idea of entire ancient Indian ethos popularized by various Upanishads. Self is indeed very thematic focus of all Upanishads which suggest that core of any person is not the body, nor the mind, nor the lower ego but only and only Atman, the spiritual essence in all human beings, their real innermost essential self.

> *"I am other than name, form and action. My nature is ever free! I am Self, the supreme unconditioned Brahman. I am pure Awareness, always non-dual".* — Adi Shankara

6

Yoga, Pranayam and Meditation
Traditional Tools and Techniques

Traditional tools of Yoga, Pranayam and Meditation have been practiced in India over thousands of years and have since spread the world over, albeit in different forms and formats. Practices of "Yogasana," the physical practice of postures, along with Meditation are well known tools used to alienate undesired routines and habits. Yoga enables us to take time to look at ourselves in the present and explore positive patterns in ourselves. It also plays a very important role in the refinement of 'Self'. It is finally through yogic asanas, pranayama and meditation that the body, mind, vital force and intellect are properly nurtured which results in shining of higher self. As a by-product, Yoga also enhances self-esteem, self-confidence and self-respect of its practitioners. Yoga helps a lot in improving practitioner's overall personality. With each foray into our inner world, through practicing Yoga, Pranayam and meditation, we become conscious of the hidden aspects of our personality.

Before going to Yoga, as a practice, it is essential to comprehend summary of Yoga Philosophy. Under the main philosophy of yoga, in a simplified way, the entities of mind, body, and spirit all come together to form a unified unique unit where individual components need not be looked as separate from each other. A multitude of philosophical ideas are used to explore the deeper dimensions of body, mind, and spirit in holistic way. Studying and understanding these ideas are essential to shift our view from being separate to the one united with Absolute Consciousness.

The Yoga philosophy believes that spiritual ignorance creates suffering and binds human beings to the wheel of samsara (cycle of rebirth). The removal of that very ignorance revolves around the practice of mental discernment, non-attachment, spiritual knowledge, and self-awareness. The law of karma is central to the philosophy of yoga. Karma is said to perpetuate our suffering and the delusion of *maya*, the illusion, the ignorance that creates the veil between our ego and our unitive connection with the universe. Yoga recognizes Brahman as the Absolute reality or Supreme reality, generally understood as the God, while the Atman, the individual spirit, or soul is called 'self'. Yoga is the science of uniting of the individual self (Atman) with the highest self (Brahman). Yoga philosophy also incorporates the concepts of the subtle body and the spiritual energies of prana and kundalini moving through the *nadis* and *chakras*.

Let us now look at each of the component of Traditional Tools in desired depth.

A. Practicing Yoga

At its core, yoga facilitates long-lasting life change through knowing ourselves better and paving strong foundation for our emotional, physical, mental and most importantly, spiritual wellbeing. Yoga helps us improve our self-understanding and allows living an empowered and fulfilling life. Yoga lets its practitioners understand themselves at a deeper level by letting them realize their unique personality, preferences, and purpose of living this life. Yoga also helps in sharpening mindful observation of daily habits and routines. As a disclaimer, Yoga being discussed here is not the normal routine associated with its current image involving sitting in some difficult postures or bending body parts in peculiar shapes.

Yoga is a very comprehensive system with its own philosophy, theory, recommended and prohibited practices, multiple stages, practices, forms, variations, and mixed adaptations. Main purpose of efforts at this moment is to touch all its aspects in brief to induce healthy inquisitiveness among readers triggering their motivation to pursue their individual exploration of Yoga in line with their passion. Yoga works as a purifier of all critical mental and physical systems. Yoga intends to remove the dirt clogging original self of its practitioner. Practicing right Yoga on regular basis sharpens observation for every part of body as well as entire surroundings. This helps a person in becoming keen observant and deeply thoughtful. One becomes the 'seer' explained under the section related to Awareness in place of 'doer'.

In our ignorant incarnation, pressures of normal life keep us away from knowing about our self, due to lack of focus and attention, or due to preconceived assumptions and stereotypes about the world. Practicing Yoga resolves all such wrong notions and bring excellent transformation of mammoth proportions. On a physical level, Yoga dredges out dirt hidden in the substratum of our systems through systematic cleaning. Yoga is known to remove the toxins and blockages, cleans and purifies breathing channels, wakes up human senses and invigorates them with clean energy. On mental level, Yoga also clears the channels of thinking and perceptions, which gives us a unique opportunity to experience things differently. Advance level Yoga is also known to remove the delusion and ignorance enveloping individual soul by resolving the adverse impact of gunas.

Yoga is of various types and newer versions are getting added by the day. In its classical form, Yoga is called Ashtanga Yoga or Raja Yoga as well as Classical Yoga. There are other popular forms designed to suit individual mental, psychological and spiritual orientations to help every person take a path of their liking to reach same final destination. The most popular of these are Karma Yoga, Jnana Yoga and Bhakti Yoga. As against these ancient variations, modern days adaptations of popular Yoga are hybrid in character as they make use of mixed features of other forms. Some of the newer forms have gained traction in recent times due to their own suitability for younger disciples going for particular aspects or attractions.

There is yet another important stream of Yoga named Tantra Yoga. Most significant names under this mixed category are Hath Yoga and Kundalini Yoga. But, out of all its forms and types, Ashtanga Yoga propagated by Maharishi Patanjali in its purer form with all the steps practiced and mastered one after another, remains the anchor for our primary focus. Ashtanga Yoga is foundational in nature and bulk of its 'dos' and 'don'ts' or asanas are used by all other Yoga variations in varying proportions.

Ashtanga Yoga gets its name as there are eight distinct steps or stages to be climbed one after another but only after mastering the lower step in entirety. So, these eight steps work like a ladder. Ultimate goal of Ashtanga Yoga is to gain sustained state of super consciousness, the quintessential stage of human evolution, called by names like Moksha or Samadhi. In Indian context Yoga was designed for the transcendence of the mind to realize the "true self" or "highest self", which very well coincide with specific purpose under our perusal.

Perfecting Yams (Don'ts) and Niyams (Dos)

Ashtanga Yoga considers Yams and Niyams as initial but cardinal steps for uplifting moral and ethical behavior to a level conducive for practicing Asanas and subsequent steps. Yams refer to prescribed prohibitions, what a noble person should not do with others, the recommended self-restraints. Underlying idea is to end all sorts of negative thoughts towards everyone and everything of the external world. On the other hand, Niyams provide for essential recommendations prescribed for a Yogi to gain inner strength, clarity and discipline to properly move forward on his spiritual journey. Let us look at each of these in some detail.

Yams (Don'ts)

The very first Yam is about strictly practicing Ahimsa, the non-violence which is best understood as freedom from harming others in any way. Actually, Ahimsa is much more than Non-violence as it includes shunning away from every action, word or thought that directly or indirectly actually harms or carry the risk of harming others. To the very least, it is the ethical and moral principle of not causing pain or injury to other living beings. Life is regarded as sacred, and tendencies of fear or weakness are said to cause violence in behavior. Showing mercy for all creatures, practicing forgiveness, abstaining from act of cruelty are all logical extensions of this very Yam. For very obvious reasons, abstaining from eating meat also emerges from this prohibition.

Second Yam theoretically restraints desire to take away things belonging or useful to others. Most writers refer it as principle of freedom from stealing, which is but a limited expansion of this critical Yam. Its real dimension is about sustaining life with a minimalist approach. Under this concept, plucking fruit from the tree violates the principle while a hungry man picking a ripe fruit already fallen at the ground qualify as acceptable. As an extension, instances like making a person wait after giving appointment or taking credit of someone's idea, also gets prohibited as part of this Yam. This prohibition directly stands diametrically opposite the life of a materialist.

This self-restraint indirectly asks to cultivate sense of self-sufficiency in whatever you are blessed with while maintaining respect for others. Holding the sense of gratitude, this Yam calls for living a simple life with contentment. Avoiding the pain of acquiring and holding excess inventory, getting rid of efforts required for maintaining its possession, sufferings from pains of allurement of its glow, undergoing pains of attachment, avoiding cravings for having more, and freedom from inevitable fear of losing a thing, are all aspects that get protected by practicing this restraint.

Thinking loudly, each of these activities leads to nagging excitations and mental disturbances, making human mind distracted. Such distractions are known to interfere the process of self-exploration. A person interested in pursuing Yoga for spiritual gains will have to see through materialism without any option. People of wisdom in past have concluded that possessions of all types and forms are sheer means and can never be justifiable ends by themselves. Further, ends are always more important than means. Allow this realization to completely sink in your internal system.

Next Yam calls for abstaining from speaking any lie in substance and all its forms. 'Satyam Vada', total truthfulness for every word spoken, is one of the strongest mantras from the Upanishads. Truthfulness encompasses basic honesty and transparency in character, conduct and all such other aspects of life. Truth is considered vital and not to be compromised even when truth may hurt feelings of another beings. Let every word spoken avoid deception or falsehood, by all means.

This Yam asks us to always apply three filters before words flow out. Those filters are, Is it true? Is it kind? Is it necessary? Let there be no word uttered without the answer to all three questions being in affirmation. Besides being truthful in words, Satya implies total commitment to truth in being, in actions and even in intentions. This Yam demands maintaining purity of mind and honesty with self. Deep-down Truth is always rock solid, clear like a daylight; it is always genuine and authentic.

Fourth Yam demands life of Brahmacharya which means not overindulging in many things like food and sex. As per classical wisdom, Brahmacharya is generally understood for its emphasis on Celibacy. Theoretically it means divine or ultimate path. Conceptually in Indian religious context, it means to stay in conduct within one's own self. However, in yoga it is applied as sensually moderate behavior. It means exercising total control over body and mind following ascetic means. Living life of Brahmacharya helps in conserving 'Ojas', the vital energies considered necessary for self-purification. Ojas means vitality, vigor and virility. Ayurveda calls it special substance in body that governs radiance, aging, immunity, vigor as well as spirituality. Ojas is the oil that brightens our lamp of life; this is what upgrades illumination to brightness.

Vachaspati Misra, Indian philosopher of the Advaita Vedanta tradition, prescribed abstention from eight types of sexual activities as a part of celibacy. These include thinking, talking, joking about sex, passionately looking at the opposite sex, secretly talking about sex, planning to engage in sexual intercourse, attempting to do so and actually doing it. One has to stay away from each of these eight activities to protect Brahmacharya.

Last Yam suggests growing non-attachment. It is common knowledge that all forms of bonds and attachments agitate human mind. Attachment brings selfishness. Charms and temptations of attachments are too strong to let go. That is why non-attachment turns out yet another critical prohibition. It basically means withdrawing attention from desires and reficussing energy on purity of thoughts and actions. A non-attached persongains freedom over bonds with things, people and concepts. Non-attachment has always been considered a highly desirable virtue and has been promoted by all home grown religious streams from India. A non-attached person gets blessed with positive behavior enabling him to act with authenticity, elegance and compassion.

Niyams ("DO's")

The very first Niyam is *Saucha*, total purity of body and mind. It actually operates on multiple levels like clean personal hygiene, well organized and clean-living space, clean thinking, and even company of clean people. By following high level of Saucha, one achieves clarity in thoughts and inspiration to be good on all levels.

Second Niyam talks about practicing contentment. Contentment is a secret ingredient of happiness. It implies respecting the reality of present; it is acceptance of situation as it exists. It is appreciation and gratitude of what you are blessed with. Contentment brings peace of mind and positivity in attitude which facilitate person's growth. Idea is not to indulge in satisfying desires but to accept life as it exists and cherish each moment by remaining grateful in whatever comes one's way.

Third Niyam is about *Tapas*, which literally means 'heat' but practically imply most strict level of 'discipline'. In Yoga, Tapas means internal flame of motivation, which brings a person to Yoga mat everyday pushing aside all the discomforts. It refers to determination for carrying out the goals and dreams. Tapas refers to going through discomfort associated with breaking habitual thinking and behavioral patterns to effect positive transformation in life. At extreme level, tapas also get stretched into self-denial of even basic physical requirements like food and sleep. Endurance being the key ingredient of Tapas, it includes every practice that pushes the mind against its own limits, for example, fasting for days, remaining awake for days at stretch, standing on one foot for days and weeks, or some such exotic and extreme exercises. Tapas gets practiced by developing perseverance and most strict self-discipline by regularly opting for fasting and penance.

Next Niyam commands *svadhyaya*, becoming self-aware with self-study. "Knowing oneself," is one of the foundational practices of yoga. Svadhyaya means the study of ancient texts, as well as the study of oneself. Idea is to reflect on writings, thoughts and actions of people of wisdom from earlier years. Later, acquired knowledge get coupled with findings of reflections and the same is used for bringing positive changes in future actions. Taking time to reflect quietly on your day through contemplation or writing personal journal is a wonderful part of practicing svadhyaya. When you delve into the wisdom of the ancients, and bravely dive into the depths of your own soul, you get direct access to all your triggers for desires, inherent intentions, and deepest fears which otherwise prevent you from feeling free in your thoughts, words and actions.

The last of Niyam calls for complete surrender of individuality by developing trust and accepting each situation with open mind and heart. Besides above five Niyams of Patanjali, other learned persons also consider some other practices as part of Niyams including practicing modesty, charity, cognition (*mati*) and vows (*vrata*). Continued and un-wavered practice of these principles, without any exception or compromise, alone leads to assured success. Every aspirant must show proper mastery over these preparatory prohibitions and mandatory practices before expecting progress out of his Yoga Asanas.

Regular Practice of Yogic Asanas

As a third step of the eight steps process, regularly practicing of Yogic Asanas, the most obvious image associated with Yoga, undoubtedly enhances flexibility, improves strength, reduces stress level and improves blood and oxygen circulation. Scientific studies carried out in recent decades also establish few other specific benefits like strengthening of immune system, boost to improved focus, improvement in metabolism, longer hydration of spinal fluids and clearing of many unwanted body toxins among others. Practicing Asanas on a regular basis also results in better lubrication of the spine and right alignments to help in daily life activities. All yoga poses are performed in conjunction and in sync with the breath. But people with Indian roots cannot miss the bigger picture that all physical advantages of Yoga are just incidental and that fundamentally Yoga is practiced for its psychological, philosophical and spiritual advantages.

Pranayam is fourth, Pratyahara (restraint of senses from their objects) is fifth and Meditation (Samadhi) happens to be sixth step. The sequence clearly establishes the important role of Asanas and Pranayam before going for Meditation. The original system, let us not forget, mandated the practitioner to master previous stage before qualifying for the next. The Yoga Sutra, by Maharishi Patanjali states that yoga happens when the mind achieves its stillness. This mental stillness is created by bringing the body, mind, and senses into balance which, in turn, relaxes the nervous system. Asanas help in achieving stilling the body while pranayama contribute towards stilling the mind.

If Yams and Niyams prepare desired quality of soil, critical for germinating seeds of our spiritual tree, practice of Asanas and Pranayam works like regular watering so critical for ensuring desired growth of that sapling into a strong tree. Best of soil cannot support growth of the plant in isolation just as merely right watering on a bad soil do not help the tree to grow any faster. At this stage let us also quickly look at other forms of Yoga besides Ashtanga Yoga explained above in detail.

Bhakti Yoga: Bhakti Yoga is the path of channeling and transmuting our emotional nature into a higher purpose. Through prayer, worship and rituals, we surrender ourselves to a Higher Being. By developing humility, self-surrender, and the feeling of being an instrument in the hands of a Higher Source, we become free from our emotions as we begin to step into the experience of Self. Also called Devotional yoga, Bhakti is the most natural path for those who are dominantly seeking emotional fulfillment and well-being.

Bhakti Yoga uses devotion as a way of transforming emotions from negativity to pleasantness. It is like falling in love and forgetting about what is happening in the world around. The bhakta usually practices this yoga and allied meditation by visualizing, thinking and feeling that the Lord is sitting or standing before him. The bhakta pours out his heart's love, adoration, and shares his deepest thoughts and concerns with the Lord until a continual flow of awareness moves between devotee and his beloved Lord. This continuous flow of love and life force brings about a superconscious state of awareness which is generally called a mood, or bhava.

Karma Yoga: Also known as Karma Marga, Karma Yoga is taken as a spiritual practice of 'selfless actions performed for the welfare of others. It is considered an established technique for crossing over influences of one's ego. Karma refers to the universal principle of cause and effect. For a Karmayogi, right action equals to a sincere prayer. Ancient Indian texts highlight the significance of undertaking selfless deeds where the doer offers his action as a service from heart with full attention, awareness and with sense of dedication. It invokes every spiritual seeker to act according to his Dharma, without being attached to the fruits/results/consequences of his actions. As per Bhagavad Gita, Karma Yoga purifies practitioner's mind. It leads him to act according to his dharma. It invokes to undertake one's work as doing god's work, and in that sense, follow the great example of Lord Krishna in every moment of one's life. Karma Yoga is most popularized by Bhagwad Gita which promulgated selfless service to the right cause, with the right feeling and right attitude, as a form of worship and seeking spirituality leading to Moksha.

Jnana Yoga: Jnana is Sanskrit for 'Wisdom'. So, Jnana Yoga is the path for liberation through wisdom. Wisdom helps knowing true nature of reality advised through meditation, self-inquiry, and contemplation. Jnana Yoga is also defined as the 'the awareness of absolute consciousness' and is a comprehensive practice focused on self-study, Svadhyaya. Jnana Yoga practices a single-pointed meditation on a single question through self-inquiry and conscious illumination to remove the veils of illusion created by practitioner's concepts, world views, and perceptions. Being an intellectual approach, it is comparatively difficult for many to pursue this path as intellectual attainments can be easily over emphasized by a mind less developed in the concept of humility and compassion. There runs the risk that intelligent mind ends up entangling the practitioner in its own constructs and thoughts forcing the practitioner losing sight of the big goal.

The main purpose of jnana yoga is to withdraw the mind and emotions from perceiving life and oneself in a fascinated way so that one may behold and live life dully tuned with Reality. One way that the yogi of discernment meditates is to patiently release or put aside all thoughts and feelings until the luminous glow of the soul dawns in the mind and heart and is allowed to do work of transformation and enlightenment within the captivated meditator.

Third Eye Yoga: This practice of Yoga directs life force of the practitioner to bring his mind and emotions so into balance that the attention gets focused on the object of contemplation directly. Generally, life force, prana is directed to move up and down the spine until it is balanced, and the mind and emotions are serenely content. Then awareness is directed to move forward into a point in the center of the lower forehead. This point is called Ajana, the third eye. When the energy is balanced throughout the brain and body and easily moving forward in the area of the third eye, practitioner's mind is said to have attained desired calmness, that is, mind remains active but free of meaningless thoughts, worries, and usual stuff of the subconscious mind. All other aspects of Ashtanga Yoga apply more or less to this Yoga also.

Tantra Yoga: As per Indian traditions, the word Tantra has many literal meanings like text, theory, system, method, instrument, technique or practice. In modern context, we should understand it as an inner technology, a sort of subjective method. Over years, the word Tantra came to represent some unorthodox methods that are not socially acceptable. While it was a just and pure path, some people used it's not so good parts and Tantra ended up earning a bad name for itself. But such false labels attached are completely ill founded and must be comprehended with neutral approach of learning because tantra, on a larger scale, provides modern context for many individual Yoga practices and techniques in vogue at present.

Tantra yoga is a relatively modern revamping of the ancient Vedic and Yogic practices. Its initiators developed innovative but unorthodox techniques to help its practitioner experience the reality of his inner Self in unity with the entire cosmos. Tantra Yoga saw value of human body as a tool to explore inward rather than expanding one's awareness outwards. It may be seen that in case of traditional Yoga systems explained before, yoga systems were centered around abandoning the physical body making very conscious efforts to detach the same from its senses, pains and sufferings. As against that, Tantra explored body's awareness and delight in the inner world of energy of the body to overcome compulsive and cyclical nature of the body and mind from working as barriers for spiritual seeking. Tantra system aimed to go beyond such that the same compulsive nature does not remain trapped as a limiting factor. Tantra Yoga focused on learning the use of body as a steppingstone to help the practitioner achieve his highest possible dimension of being human. In Tantra Yoga, the subtle bodies of energy and spirit are developed to facilitate crossing from physical to the Divine. Its method focuses on the purification and cultivation of life breath to activate all the Kundalinis.

Tantra uses the physical body to activate energy using practices of asanas, pranayama, mudras (gestures made using hands) and shatkarma (esoteric exercises and techniques to purify the body and cleanse the energy pathways). These are same asanas and pranayama which is very commonly used today while practicing Hath Yoga, an off shoot of Tantra Yoga itself. The Yogi aims at expanding all levels of his consciousness to uncover the curtain from hidden Supreme Reality. To that respect, Tantra uses Shakti, the dynamic aspect of divinity also called 'The Cosmic Mother'. The practitioner aims to release his subconscious blockages using spiritual dynamic energy to transform his personal limitations. Although, larger aim of Tantra was always to awaken and harmonize both male and female aspects present within each individual as an expression of Shakti, some perverted natured people misconstrued tantra's symbolism into sex practices bringing it very bad name.

Hath Yoga: Hatha yoga, in current times, mainly practiced for health and vitality, is basically an extension of Tantra itself as the Asanas, Pranayama and Meditation practices overlap almost completely. Being largely physical, Hath Yoga captured attention of West so much that Yoga in West inadvertently means Hath Yoga by default. Hatha yoga was brought to America by Swami Vivekananda in 1893 as a spiritual practice. Beginning the 1920s, various yogis from India started going to West and began combining asanas with other popular exercises of the day created a flowing style of yoga that was more physical than spiritual. In a way, it was need of the hour because for appreciation of the spiritual aspect necessitated comprehension and belief in original Yoga philosophy, which was almost an impossible task considering the deep gulf of Western and Eastern cultures. Hath yoga gained fast acceptance and popularity riding on its direct and visible benefits towards making the body flexible and healthy. Yogic exercises got accepted as vital instrument for unique impacts for body, mind and soul. Its physical advantages are quantifiable and it also helps in improving mental faculties like concentration.

Finally, let us look at how Yoga, in all its forms and variations, helps strengthening morality and ethics. Yoga and ethics need to be taken as intrinsic rather than mere complimentary to each other. Let us also remember that ethics and morality are not issues of reason or intellect but a matter of practice, an understanding that comes only to actual practitioners. Practicing yoga encourages strict discipline in food, sleep, work, enjoyment and such other activities involved in living normal life. Thus, entire way of life gains traction for the better.

Role of Teachers in Practicing Yoga

Yoga is best learned, at least in the initial stages, under guidance of a learned Yoga Teacher. There are many types of yoga and depending on one's mental and psychological make-up, different Yoga forms may appeal to a beginner. The very first contribution from a trained Yoga teacher is to keenly observe learner's personality and identify his starting point so that there is no mismatch in learner's basic nature and the kind of Yoga he practices.

Later, the teacher can also help you navigate through sequence of postures, breathing exercises, and contemplations. Practicing different asanas demands minute level observations which only an independent observer is better placed to critically watch. Expecting any individual to observe his own subtle nuances from start to finish of any single posture including breathing sequence etc. are just too much. A teacher is best placed to pinpoint the areas of mistakes and improvements required.

A certified Yoga instructor is also helpful to you to modify your poses and offer suggestions wherever required. Besides attending to all your potential questions with ready replies, a Yoga teacher also has a role in helping you remain in present. The most important role for a trained Yoga teacher is through his knowledge of anatomy and physiology which helps him develop a keen eye for proper alignment in the postures helping you practice without compromising all important safety.

B. Practicing Pranayam Regularly

"Prana" is Breath or vital energy for the body. On subtle levels "prana" represents the energy responsible for life. Ayama, on the other hand, can be translated as expansion or dimension. So, pranayama is Expansion of Breath or expanded dimensions of life force. Maharishi Patanjali mentioned Pranayam in his famous Yoga Sutras as means of attaining higher states of awareness. There are different types of Pranayam but 'four times four' method is considered as one of the basic Pranayam practice.

This practice requires breathing-in spreading over four seconds of time, holding the breath for full four seconds, exhaling slowly spreading over another four seconds, and finally holding on empty again for four seconds. Few cycles of this routine are an established method for regulating breathing, balancing the moods and pacifying the body under most situations. In addition, there are endless variations of breath regulation involving varying combinations of sequencing, intensity, time spent and number of cycles of respective pranayama. Sustained practice of routines consisting of multiple variations are practiced to obtain assured physical and spiritual benefits.

The routine popularized by Swami Ramdev of Patanjali Yogapeeth is also accepted as an excellent starting point for the beginners. The most popular eight breathing exercises recommended and popularised by Swami Ramdev include Bhastrika, Kapalbhati, Bahaya, Ujjai, Anulom Vilom, Bharamari, Udgeetha and Pranav. Many practitioners also report of evolving their own variations of routines overtime, which in a way also help in dealing with the monotony of following a set routine over very long period. Periodic variations also help in letting practitioner know what works better for him at different stages of his long practice. For the minimum duration, however, the whole process should not be practiced for less than twenty minutes to begin with. Later, with experience under the belt, the time for practice may be increased further to about 45 minutes per sitting.

Within overall Yoga umbrella, pranayama is used along with Asanas and Meditation. Combining all three practices is said to deliver final benefits envisaged out of Yoga in total. But pranayama, on its own, as a standalone practice, also has benefits of immense proportions. These advantages arise in terms of therapeutic effects through controlled breathing. In the process, as in case of Asanas, Pranayam also delivers its own physical benefits like reduced blood pressure, increased immunity, improved lung functions, reduction in stress, and reduction in anxiety for the long run. It brings balance among *doshas* of *Vata, Pitta* and *Kapha* resulting in significant health benefits.

As part of mental benefits, Pranayam makes mind steady and calm. As a very first step, it augments supply of oxygen to the mind resulting in drastic reduction of stress levels. Regular practitioners of Pranayam report increased mental alertness and heightened feeling of exhilaration. Regular practice of pranayama keeps temptations at bay and throws out the negativity and impulsive responses out of your system. It is an excellent exercise for keeping mind cheerful over long periods and maintaining higher levels of enthusiasm and energy for all of its practitioners. On the psychic level, Pranayam allows introversion of mind paving way for subsequent activities relating to self-awareness, self-observation, self-acceptance and finally self-realization. The loop of *'study to practice to perfection—to study to practice and further perfection'* remains true for years together. Pranayam is advisable on empty stomach only. Morning time is always considered ideal for practicing Pranayama. But just like Yoga, any other time suitable always prove as second-best option. Body cleaned, stomach at rest, physical body fully relaxed, and composed state of mind, are advisable preparations before sitting for every Pranayam session.

Morality induced by practicing Yoga and Pranayama is indeed true morality as it accrues from purification of consciousness. Morality originated from inside, under guidance of pure consciousness, certainly emerge foundational in nature and unwavering in character. True that results from Yoga and Pranayama induced moral upliftment may not be visible to a naked eye but as and when these accrue, they are rock solid and bring transformational support to our practice of meditation. All above benefits also mirror exactly same for Understanding self, our specific purpose on hand,

Another area where Pranayam has great impact is our thinking process. The link between breathing and thinking is both direct and deep. As per Ayurveda, process of contemplation consists of two distinct parts, physical and psychological, where breathing is physical part while thinking is its psychological sibling. Obviously, the second is conditional to the presence of the first. Pranayam takes care of both breathing and thinking. During pranayama routines, breath is skillfully inhaled, exhaled and retained like a symphony at work. It leads to perfect relief from physical and mental tensions arising due to breathing. Indeed, Pranayam brings you closer to your Self and helps you to be with it for longer durations.

C. Practicing Meditation

Practicing meditation is the journey starting from 'Selfishness' and going up to 'Selflessness' and finally to Universal oneness. Awakening the mind to new realities or a paradigm shift is important for excelling in many fields like arts, sports, or crafts etc. An awakened person, on spiritual path also, applies these qualities to gain discerning wisdom and intuitive ability by gaining profound insights in his own heart and mind. Later, with practice, some more practice, and refinements, one can expect to get awakened to higher truths and transcendental reality beyond this visible world. But called by names like self-aware or self-realized, awakening to our very core, this expedition has always been considered as a higher goal of humanity.

You may call it art or science but what meditation does is to help in living a fulfilling human life by enabling access to many tools one develops, and works with, to live a conscious existence. This consciously awakened life is not for improving unknown after life but for actual ongoing human life, here and now, by bringing required transformation through enhancing virtues of love, empathy and energy. This awakening enhances the equanimity to accept what is beyond control. Most importantly, the awakening provides us required intellect to identify the difference between such control and acceptance. Once perfected, knowledge about self also helps us to be aware at our deepest level beyond our usual divisions and segregations. Thus, meditation is that most effective tool to help us reach the pinnacle of our living experience.

Speaking in practical terms, Meditation is sum of all techniques and systems deployed for achieving transformation of mind aimed at developing a stage of consciousness where the mind is free from all scattered thoughts, patterns, conflicts and divisions; where the mind can develop focus, bring clarity of thoughts, establish emotional balance and gain ability to see things in their pure form. At advance level, meditation is called the art of achieving conscious state of mind. At that level Meditation requires a state of mind like stillness of water in a clean lake where even a single leaf lying at its bottom surface is visible from above and a single ripple on the top surface is easily traced to its point of origin.

"Our concern in meditation is to know oneself, not only superficially, but the whole content of the inner, hidden consciousness. Without knowing all that and being free

> *of its conditioning, you cannot possibly go beyond the mind's limits. That is why the thought process must cease, and for this cessation there must be knowledge of oneself. Therefore, meditation is the beginning of wisdom, which is the understanding of one's own mind and heart."* — Jiddu Krishnamurti

Practicing Meditation generates great deal of impurity and dirt accumulated in untrained minds. Settling down of all those impurities happen ever so slowly where meditation works as a cleansing process. Off course, this process need be supported by other 'off-the-mat' activities like improved compassion, empathy, morality and ethics. Meditation being a completely voluntary practice, one must mindfully watch the mud swirl without any force or repression.

The equipment and laboratory used in Meditation is one's own mind. Success in meditation requires work on two fronts. Firstly, for reprocessing of impressions, experiences, memories accumulated from past and secondly by installing a strong security system for regulating entry of negative or undesired thoughts at present. Thus, meditation is more about training and regulating the mind, a process which requires one climbing his own Mount Everest. That is why each practitioner has his own stories about time taken, progress made, techniques used, obstacles dealt with and general ups and downs faced all through their meditation journey.

Taking it as a systematic training to withdraw thoughts from the external world and observe, analyze, regulate and finally reflect on them after gaining inward focus, is another way of understanding meditation. Over long periods, this process results in mind's accumulated mental content duly reflected, removing layers of false perceptions one by one. This purity and clarity allow inward focus of mental attention for finally inducing sense of active consciousness. To achieve this global objective, there are host of philosophies, tools, techniques, practices, and methods. Each of these techniques have their own origin geography, time, cultural and religious moorings.

For people familiar with game of Cricket, practicing meditation is like regular batting practice with bowling machine. There are no score cards, no run chase, no spectators, no umpires and no selectors on the scene. You decide your own time window and take the opportunity to learn and perfect your own techniques without anybody watching or having any interest as to how you go about it. This makes it fairly a boring and unattractive activity. But when you are on the field, same practice helps you perform better but without any surety. Benefits expected from practicing meditation fall in physical, mental, social, emotional, psychological and spiritual domains and begin to accrue just after initial few sessions and keep increasing with intensification of practice which goes for years and years. However, the ultimate spiritual advancement, the stage critical for our process of Understanding Self, accrues only after prolonged practice requiring concentrated efforts, dedication and determination.

Making a clean beginning in your practice need sorting out of many issues. Setting a suitable time schedule comes first of preparation. Having sessions at same time daily aids in mental focus. One may have to reschedule other activities in the process. Paucity of time is reported by many people as the problem stopping them from starting meditation. Sharing out of personal experience, meditation is a time neutral practice or leaves you with more time because it makes you capable of performing at higher productivity levels during the day.

Next preparation is about the place to be used for meditation. Finding a cozy corner, and that too within comforts of your own home, works out a winner for practical reasons. The corner selected should not be noisy. Since the place soon develops an aura of its own, you are advised not to change your place very often. Later, all you need is a clean and pious place away from distractions of all types.

Pledging for perpendicular posture comes next in getting ready. Right posture is a must for proper meditation. Proven empirically, Lotus Asana is best posture for meditation. What you need to ensure is keeping your back, neck and head in erect posture. This is critical because in this posture alone your mind receives least sensations from various body parts. No other posture meets this requirement as good as Lotus or half lotus postures. Settling length of your sessions and beholding your breath are some other issues you have to deal before getting ready for your daily meditational sessions. After settling all the preparatory issues, you begin to focus on your mental content and it is there that several techniques need be explored alternatively.

Next most critical part is that of breathing. Mastery in Pranayam become essential for appropriately shaping breathing to facilitate effective meditation. For smooth meditation, your breath must be shaped well to ensure that it is deep, smooth, even, without sound, without pause and has very tender transition between inhaling and exhaling. Pranayam involves systematic working on change in depth of breathing, changes in rate of breathing and most importantly at varying patterns of breathing. Only a practitioner with years invested in his practice knows challenges faced in establishing proper rhythm in respirations such that the breathing during meditation can avoid all known adjectives like being labored, unlabored, gasping, too fast, too slow, too deep or wheezing. Perfecting Pranayam routines achieves that very purpose.

Meditation Techniques and Practices

"Meditation should not be regarded as a learning process. It should be regarded as an experiencing process where you try not to learn from it but try to feel it. Meditation is an act of non-duality where techniques you use should not be separate from you; it is you, you are the technique. Meditator and Meditation are one. There is no relationship involved."

— Chogyaam Trungpa Rinpoche, Tibetan Buddhist Meditation master

Practitioners of meditation have varying mental orientations and need different practices to pursue. There are tons of techniques available for practicing meditation which differ from each other on many counts, sometimes standing in opposite corners from each other. For example, there is a silent technique and another asking for chanting mantras; some suggest focus on physical objects while other prefer focus on abstract thoughts. Some suggest regulation of mental processes while other allow it to roam freely. Few rely on time tested ancient techniques while others see merit in trying newer experimental methods. And for this harmless secular practice, we got another list of divisions based on links with traditions, cultures and beliefs, one belongs to.

In reality, however, different meditation techniques are like traces of trails available to innocent climber to explore the landscape of his mountain with the aim of advancing towards the peak. Those trails appear going in different directions while crisscrossing at irregular distances. Some run parallel for some distance before either merging or forking out. Some look hard to walk initially but turn smooth after a while, and vice versa. Still, all one got is all those trails. Techniques are means and not ends. Different person finds different types giving different results at different stages of their practice. No technique be called superior to others. A practitioner is better off by trying different techniques and find out what works for him. Techniques for meditation are like scaffolding support required for constructing a grand structure. Once building is over, same scaffolding gets dumped in some corner without much thought.

Let us briefly touch some of the more popular techniques originating on Indian soil. The order of their sequence is just a random as there is no firm basis to categorize them in any fix order.

***Vipassana Meditation*:** Vipassana is a way of transforming self through pure observation and bringing focus on deeper connection of body and mind. It is in fact revival of the ancient technique conforming to teachings of Buddha. This practice is learnt over ten days course where participants have to remain within the defined area having no contact with the rest of the world. During this period all one does is to follow instructors' advice. Participants practice mental concentration for first few days before being introduced to Vipassana proper. Other steps are rolled out one by one such that by end of the course entire process get laid out in open. The technique requires practitioners to make full efforts without any pressure but this simple rule itself offers its own challenges, especially in the beginning.

By the end of ten days camp, most people report their ability in making effortless efforts to sustain a relaxed alertness along with detached involvement. Later, after mastering access concentration, the attention is turned to objects of practice, which normally are thoughts and sensations. One is supposed to observe awareness without attachment, letting thoughts and sensations arise and pass away on their own accord. It is an easy to learn practice where plenty of reading material and audio/videos supports are easily available.

***Mindful Meditation*:** As per Buddhist teachings, mindfulness is used to develop self-knowledge and wisdom that leads to freedom from all kinds of sufferings. Mindfulness technique is to intentionally focus on present moment, accepting and non-judgmentally paying attention to sensations or thoughts. Actually, it can be practiced for the most mundane jobs of daily life as well. As per this practice, anything done mindfully becomes meditation, provided you retain your attention on that activity, and bringing it back again on the same object as soon as you notice it flying out. The other condition is to observe your thoughts, feelings and emotions without following them or entertaining them in any way. You need to be 'aware' of them but not 'being into them'.

***Mantra Meditation*:** A mantra is a sacred utterance, a numinous sound, a syllable, believed to be having psychological and spiritual powers. Sounds, vibrations, along with speed and rhythm, have profound impact on body, mind and emotions. Mantra meditation uses these effects with ultimate objective of calming, decontaminating and transforming the mind and heart of the practitioner. Mantra is said to be much powerful than the literal meaning of the words comprising a mantra. Mantra draws power from conviction and belief of the chanter.

One can chose a mantra for himself or get it from the Guru. There being no restriction on length, a mantra can be a single word or a small poem, for that matter. The practitioner must feel comfortable and happy in reciting the mantra over and over without losing interest. Ultimately, the selected mantra becomes the anchor of entire practice. Every word of the mantra must be pronounced with right emphasis on each syllable and the meaning of each word must be fully sucked up each time a mantra is recited. Also important is to synchronize speed and decibels with breathing (which is linked to state of mind of that moment). One can be as loud as sustainable in the beginning but later all mantras are best recited in the mind.

Staring Meditation: This is also a one-pointed meditation where we stare on a single object placed in front. The object can be anything like a symbol, idol, picture, candle flame or just a small black dot. This meditation accentuates desirable combination of power of concentration and stilling of mind. In due course of the practice, the gaze becomes stronger and stronger, such that, everything other than object of choice gets blacked out. At that stage, the benefits like enhanced intuition, reduced distractions, and increased energy start accruing in visible manner. As an alternate to external object, one may as well decide to use internal imagination. That way this practice can also be carried out with closed eyes. In this case, the choice of object can be endless as one can select a thing of past, of any dimension, living or dead, etc. The philosophy remains same, that is, to become one with the object.

Kundalini Meditation: Kundalini meditation has its roots in Tantra Yoga. Kundalini is said to be a bundle of latent energy lying dormant in the shape of a coiled serpent located at the base of spine. Tantra assumes that fabric of human life is made of several layers of *nadis*, subtle currents continuously flowing energies through the body. There are three principal *nadis*, named as Sushumna, Ida and Pingala, going through the spinal cord and the chakras: the energy centers of the body. Asanas, Pranayam, and chanting are said to be the most common ways to move prana around the body via these *nadis*. These currents are weaved and re-weaved in an integrated manner is the conceptual belief in tantric traditions. It suggests that accumulated dormant potential can be awakened by a difficult process involving opening of each of the seven Chakras. Those Chakras are said to be located at specific places within upper body starting from the spinal base going all the way up to the crown in the skull. Tantra demands that as human beings it is our obligation to access the broadest range of powers and privileges bestowed upon us and use them with great responsibility.

According to Tantra school, the natural life forces that pervade through the universe are assimilated through our Chakras, the psychic centers. It is believed that consciousness intersects with flow of energy at each of the Chakra. Normal human body is said to have over fifty different places of Chakras but awakening of Kundalini involves only significant seven Chakras, out of which five are located across the spine and remaining two in the brain area. The Chakras are generally depicted as little wheels of energy holding invisible energy fields together. The practice of Meditation for awakening Kundalini focuses attention on one Chakra at a time starting from the base. The coiled energy at the base is regarded as primal in nature and very powerful in its impact. Awakening of the Kundalini leads to profound conscience and ultimate bliss.

In addition, as per ancient Indian texts, there are 72000 *nadis* interconnecting through ethers within and around our physical bodies. The subtle body around our physical bodies is called the aura. All the nadis work like physical bodies running through our nervous system. Sushumna is like body's great river flowing from the base of the spine to the crown of the head. The ida and pingala nadis spiral around the sushumna nadi like the double helix of our DNA, crossing each other at every Chakra. As per Kundalini system, exercising around these seven specific psychic centers goes a long way in bringing regulation within our physical bodies.

Awakening of Kundalini is said to be an effective system of cleansing entire body and mind combine for getting rid of all tensions and stresses accumulated within the subconscious system due to all types of emotional and psychological processes going on and on in normal human life. But, as a general disclaimer, the entire concept of Tantra, Kundalini and Chakras is full of scientifically unproven assumptions and working around these involves great amount of belief, discipline and efforts which is an independent subject matter.

However, Kundalini Yoga is neither about invoking some sort of magic nor following any belief system. It is simply a technique driven practice that uses mind, senses and body to establish unique communication within self, body and mind. A kundalini awakening is not so much a physical force, but the movement of the energy of the subtle body. Therefore, one should not attempt the awakening without taking the right steps to open and purify the channels of the subtle body. Even in recent times, one finds many teachers and centers focused entirely on the Tantra Yoga and many people confirm experiencing awakening of their Kundalini.

Most recommended Kundalini Meditation practice requires attention focus on three major Chakras located at Heart, Third eye and Crown locations. While undertaking meditation sessions, the practitioner must focus and redirect his attention to the selected center as a means of silencing the thought process with the aim of enlarging gaps, in between alternate thoughts, as much as possible. Most prominent of all the Chakras is the Third Eye Chakra located in between the eyebrows. With Sanskrit name Ajna, as per yogic metaphysics this Chakra is the center where one transcends duality, where I-consciousness is absorbed into super-consciousness. In psychological and behavioral characteristics, this Chakra navigates vision, intuition, perception, access to mystical states and connection with wisdom. Third eye chakra works as an instrument to process the more subtle qualities of reality. Its awakening directly opens an intuitive sensibility and inner perception and thereby guides entire process of spiritual growth.

***Yoga Meditation*:** Yoga meditation works as a broad umbrella covering multiple techniques within its aegis. As already discussed under Yoga chapter, its initial practice involves strictly following rules of moral conduct, mastering physical postures, and regular practice of Pranayam (breath control). These limbs are followed by contemplative practices consisting of pratyahara, dharana and dhyana to ultimately reach for Samadhi. Yoga emphasizes that basic preparations over morality, personal conduct, stilling the body with the help of posture routines enable mind becoming willing and receptive for self-regulation and to focus attention on desired sound, word, organ, chakra, thought or such other object of choice. As such, these underlying principles equally apply to all practices. Similarly, all practices under Yoga Meditation never aim to stop the mind or make it go blank. It is because Yoga philosophy believes that effort to stop the mental activity or to forcefully bring it under regulation is a battle lost even before starting. Let us briefly touch some of the prominent techniques falling under Yoga.

Visual Meditation: Also known as Subjective visual Meditation, this practice requires your focus on a visual image inside your mind. Most of us directly believe in own physical power but have doubts about mental powers. But visual cues are undoubtedly better for learning as compared to auditory or kinesthetic cues. Visuals are best suited for harnessing the energy of our imaginative powers and that is why imagery is considered most fundamental language. Yoga also suggests mental power to be more potent if applied properly. Visual meditation is the technique that uses power of human imagination for positive thinking to bring about desired results in physical forms. Incidentally, imagination or inner visualization is not a gift for select few individuals, but an attribute that is open for cultivation and perfection by everybody using determined efforts and patience.

Proven with scientific studies in recent past, imagery and visualization alleviate stress, physical pains, anxieties and such other tensions. That is why visualization, besides being meditation, is also considered as a healing therapy. Visual meditation works on the fundamental point that human minds comprehend every idea first in the shape of an image and, based on such image alone, directs various body organs to translate that into actual physical form. Sitting posture and all other preparations for other techniques apply equally here as well.

Harnessing of imaginative energy of mind is achieved by evolving positivity and influencing the body to act accordingly. While undertaking this meditation, the practitioner assumes that everything around is positive and conducive, the environment is facilitative, people around are all loving and caring. This constant imaginary, over long periods, results in complete absence of negative tendencies from thoughts and actions of the practitioner. All through this meditation, special attention remains on deep breathing which works both as a relaxation tool and a technique keeping the mind stable and receptive for positivity. For example, seeing yourself as completely healthy person in your own thoughts or visualizing the image of a healthy person, helps your mind to send strong signals to body to understand the desire and work towards it.

Kriya Meditation: According to Paramahansa Yogananda, the most vocal proponent of Kriya Yoga, it is a simple psychological method by which human blood is de-carbonated and recharged with oxygen. The atoms of this extra oxygen are transmuted into life current to rejuvenate the brain and spinal centers, The Yogi further added that by stopping the accumulation of venous blood, the practitioner is able to lessen or prevent the decay of tissues. In his autobiography, Yogananda calls Kriya technique as the revival of the same science that Krishna imparted to Arjuna millenniums ago. The Yogi quotes his guru and writes.

> *"Kriya Yoga is an instrument through which human evolution can be quickened. The ancient yogis discovered that the secret of cosmic consciousness is intimately linked with breath mastery. This is India's unique and deathless contribution to the world's treasury of knowledge. The life force, which is ordinarily absorbed in maintaining heart action, must be freed for higher activities by a method of calming and stilling the ceaseless demands of the breath."*

Paramahansa Yogananda also laid out a well-defined and well explained process of practicing Kriya Yoga asking the practitioner to direct life energy to revolve upward and downward, around six spinal centers. One-half minute of revolution of energy around the sensitive spinal cord of a person aids subtle progress in his evolution. He mentions that for people living normal materialistic life, the flow of energy is towards the outward world resulting in the wasting of currents on senses. According to Yogi, the Kriya practice reverses that very flow and guides the life force to the inner cosmos, reuniting the same with subtle spinal energies.

Kriya Yoga is an advanced level practice which requires a whole lot of ground preparation before making desired progress. The objective of this effort, here in this book, is to generate interest in the minds of readers to revisit this practice once significant progress is achieved in their meditative journey. The authority to bestow Kriya Yoga instructions and initiation of eligible students lies with Yogoda Satsang Society formed by respected Paramahansa Yogananda himself. He also provided for the perpetual dissemination of the Kriya Yoga science through Yogoda Satsang lessons available from Yogoda Satsang Society of India. Interested seekers are advised to directly get in touch with the said institution for further inquiries.

***Self-Inquiry Meditation*:** As the very name suggest, this technique is directly related to our purpose of Understanding Self. The simple sounding question of "Who am I?" remains within us in a latent state and requires tons of work on the journey of spiritual advancement before letting us make a fruitful meaning of our very own divine existence. This power of recognizing our existence remains buried deep down under the mountain full of materialistic and egoistic overburden which needs to be removed layer by layer before we get a peep into it.

'*Kleshas*' and '*Vasanas*,' or toxic desires and responses, in the form of familiar stories, emotions, self-images, beliefs, and reactive patterns keep us tied with our ego-based personality as a big curtain hiding the actual content. These known tendencies cover person's essential nature under thick layers of ignorance which need to be peeled off before accessing our shiny sun, the timeless, silent, ever-present being. This very existence is called Self by Vedanta and True nature by Zen Masters. The practice of Self-inquiry, propagated by one of the most acclaimed Indian sages of modern times, Sri Ramana Maharshi (1879-1950), is recommended only for the matured practitioners.

Like in most other meditation practices, the mind keeps flying from one thought to another in an endless manner and needs to be brought back and focused on our contemplative being. Under Self-inquiry, however, the mind is required to rest on Self, the feeling of 'I'. In a way, this practice focuses on awareness of the awareness itself such that we can cross over the forces of duality. Success of this method is said to have been achieved when the object of meditation (the 'I') ultimately gets revealed as the subject (the Transpersonal Consciousness) itself.

In this simple but powerful method, the practitioner is expected to convert his gaze into a laser beam turned inward for illuminating the path of self-inquiry permeating right through pure consciousness. The great 20th-century Advaita sage propagates an ancient path called "Atma vichara", self-inquiry. Wikipedia page on the subject defines Self-enquiry as "…. is the constant attention to the inner awareness of 'I' or 'I am' recommended by Ramana Maharshi as the most efficient and direct way of discovering the unreality of the 'I'-thought."

For sure, this method is appealing only to spiritually adventurous practitioners with years of practice behind them as underlying fundamental question does not usually bother normal beings. The names of people engulfed by this question in human history are countable few, but it does not mean others cannot have life-altering glimpse of the radiant sun of true nature. In fact, only such glimpses have the potential to free us from suffering once and for all.

As per Stephan Bodian, a psychotherapist, teacher and an internationally known author of many known books on the subject including "Beyond Mindfulness—The direct Approach to lasting Peace, Happiness and love", the twin practices of abiding (or resting) and inquiring work together like the left and right foot in walking. First, we rest in the calmness and clarity of our basic sitting practice, whatever it may be. Then, when the waters are relatively still, we inquire, and the inquiry may reveal a new level of insight into the silence and stillness of our essential nature that allows us to rest even more deeply. And from this deeper resting, we have the capacity to inquire even further."

To begin the practice of self-inquiry, Stephan Bodian advises to sit for meditation as usual. If you do not already have a regular practice, just sit quietly and allow the mind to settle naturally. Do not attempt to focus your mind or manipulate your experience, just rest as awareness itself. After 10 or 15 minutes, when the mind is relatively open and present, introduce the question "Who am I?" As you continue your self-inquiry, you may notice that the question begins to permeate your consciousness and soon you may find yourself asking it not only during meditation but at unexpected times throughout the day.

Instead of "Who am I?" you may prefer asking, "Who is thinking this thought?" Such questions direct your awareness inward, away from the external world and toward the source from which all experiences arise. Indeed, anything you can perceive, no matter how intimate, including the cluster of images, memories, feelings, and beliefs you take to be you, is merely an object of perception. Who is this entity experiencing everything? Who is the real perceiver? Who is the ultimate subject of all those objects? These are very real questions at the heart of "Who am I".

Conclusions

There are plenty of techniques with their countless variants with each offering some unique advantage. But selection of particular technique at specific stage of one's practice vary from person to person and is more a matter of 'Trial and Error'. One is strongly advised to be open for experimenting different techniques and switch over from one to another intermittently. One can, however, consider some established golden rules for making right choice of technique. The technique should be practical to adopt at each stage of your practice. It should be able to invoke serious engagement. It should also be challenging enough to bring the best out. And above all, the practice should remain enjoyable.

Finally, meditation as a practice helps us knowing our Self not only on conscious level but on unconscious and subconscious levels too. Meditation helps us in gaining clarity and neutrality about our true motives. It helps us immensely in realizing our true nature which otherwise was hidden under the overburden of colored views of being socially and morally correct viewpoints. This knowledge alone helps to acknowledge that a desire to change the world actually means making changes at one's individual level. Knowing about self is the very first step in this long journey. It helps us remove subjectivity and replaces the same with objectivity at our deeper levels. At this stage, reasoning of our actions become more reasonable and logic behind our thoughts become more logical.

Part II

7

Advanced Self
Its Philosophical Perspective

Advancing 'self' to 'Self'

Besides the obvious subjective aspects of self being physical, psychological, social and personal, there is yet another very important aspect self called as the philosophical Self or spiritual Self. This aspect relies more heavily on unique and subtle human qualities of intellect, discrimination and wisdom. Here the Self crosses known boundaries of body/mind and intellect. In Indian contexts, this aspect largely revolves around inward looking quest, which leads to ultimate truth of everything of this universe found inside the human being itself. A person mastering that is said to be a man of wisdom in his own capacity. In modern parlance, we can identify this Self with the 'superman' residing inside each of us waiting to be found, acknowledged and explored. This Self is based on subjective and qualitative experiences advocated by Ancient Indian scriptures as against the Western view focused on objective and quantitative aspects.

For the sake of simplicity, let us look at two aspects of Self under discussion called as lower and higher self. Lower self refers to undeveloped self that remains engaged in activities relating to survival and feel-good factors like eating, sleeping, procreating, enjoying luxuries etc. This self is identified as the empirical self, the existential self, which is subject to usual sorrows and sufferings both physical and intellectual. This empirical self in unstable and is subject to change at all times. On the other hand, the higher self refers to the basic premise described as eternal, omnipotent, conscious, and intelligent being, one's real self.

The true self or the Higher Self or unchanging Self, also called Atman (which can also be loosely understood as spirit or soul), that observes the empirical phenomena, is said to be unaffected and undying. Indian philosophies consider mind as a gross entity emanating from and controlled by subtler entities, where subtler of all is called Atman. True seeker of self must eventually become intimately familiar with the workings of his internal sub-systems, his 'inner equipment'. He must listen to internal voice, then rigorously contemplate upon it, and finally, use the equipment (mind) to overcome the very equipment. In another classification, Self can also be divided into three distinct categories – physical or material self, the relational self and finally the reflective or contemplative self, where the third aspect is considered as Higher Self or Purer Self.

The Higher Self merely remains a witness, abiding in its full and peaceful nature. When a person gets tired of fruitless search for enduring happiness in the subjective world, he is forced to turn inwards with determination and sincere commitment. This is when we arrive at the threshold of spirituality. When we pursue spirituality with genuine sincerity, our egocentric desires and personality starts to crumble. We gain a greater inner poise and serenity as the beauty of the Self starts to shine through. Finally, we rediscover our true nature and realize our oneness with it, which in simpler words means practical self-realization.

Understanding Atman, The True Self

Upanishads describe original quality of Atman as eternal, blissful, divine, pure, and infinite. Atman is regarded as Pure Consciousness. Atman is the core, or the essence while Ego is said to be its outer packing giving origin to sense of separateness as a unique individual. Atman is the real self but remains covered by the impurities and tempering by things of the visible world. The outer wrapper, being visible, contributes to making beings remain in delusion and ignorance from their real Self.

Due to complexities involved, a common man of modern times, finds such concepts difficult to comprehend leave alone practicing them in life. Attempts to describe the infinite through finite words make it even more difficult. Despite this, few beings remain dedicated, to know the unknown, to describe the indescribable, or to explore the infinite. Striving to capture the true Self, or Atman, is that very reflection of our spiritual nature or intellectual inquisitiveness. This is the same process that is used in all inventions and innovations, be it in the field of science, space or theology. As such, the reader is advised to remain inquisitive and patient while dealing with these issues and concepts.

> *"The word atman means: that which is your own. Regardless of how much the rest may appear to you as your own, it is alien. All of that which you otherwise claim as yours – friends, loved ones, family, wealth, fame, high position, a great empire – it is all a deception...... That which death can separate you from, know that it didn't belong to you, and that which it can't, was indeed your own."* — Osho

The Atman is supposed to express itself through the Antahkarana which is taken as the totality of two levels of mind, the first called Buddhi, the intellect or higher mind, and the second called Manas, the middle levels of mind which exist as or include the mental body. Besides these two levels, Antahkarana is also linked to Ahamkara, the Ego and Chitta, the subconscious. For better understanding, the reader is advised to consider these four aspects (Buddhi, Manas, Ahamkara and Chitta) in terms of their functions rather than in terms of distinct entities simply because there is no physical substance to any of them.

Let us begin with ahamkara as the first aspect of the Antahkarana and trying to comprehend how it relates with Self. Ahamkara, the ego alone gives us the feeling of we being limited to our body and mind. Buddhi is less subtle than Ahamkara and is responsible for making decisions and directing the Manas, which works in combination or collaboration of the five sense organs and serves as a dashboard upon which the impressions gathered by the senses are imprinted. Manas goes forth, receives impressions from the senses, sorts, and changes them into concepts based on past impressions and memories. Manas then hands these concepts over to the Buddhi, which either selects or rejects those impressions for its own contemplation.

The subconscious, Chitta, is said to be less subtle than the Ahamkara and is responsible for managing memories. As an extension of memory management, it also deals with all recollections and forgetfulness. Chitta receives knowledge from Buddhi and stores it. Antahkarana is said to operate in two modes. Firstly, it operates by looking outside and obtain external knowledge. Secondly, it can turn inward and obtain Self-knowledge. This process involves the gross going back to the subtle, where Manas involves with Ahamkara and ultimately with the Sakshi, the Atman.

The process of realizing the Witness, the Real Self, involves bypassing the mind. However, the entire process of bypassing mind requires the concentrated use of that very mind. And that is where bulk of human problems of managing the mind rest. Just imagine, a sophisticated equipment working on a software to bypass itself.

8

Tools for Advancing Higher Self

Developing best of understanding about Self shall prove useful only when it gets applied to bring required improvements in our self-concept, self-confidence, self-esteem, attitudes, aptitudes, thoughts, feelings and every such thing connected with our Self. Our understanding must help us find gaps and suggest tools to bring corrections if so required. Needless to mention that efforts required for advancing Self, being transformational in character, are indeed challenging, and demand a great deal of perseverance, commitment, and dedication.

These tools are comparable to advancing education at graduation level. These are voluntary and time consuming, and, at times, expensive too. You need to find long hours to practice them which certainly calls for balancing among other responsibilities and priorities. Practicing them bring to surface moral and ethical issues of darker shades many of which were not even confronted in earlier avatar. At college level, you decide to study your chosen subjects, you research your own pool of texts, illustrations, background information and reference material. Even when you have access to professors, they can't be approached without good preparations. Topics covered are far and few but you get no luxury to pick and choose any part of those topics just because you find them difficult or less interesting. Learning environment is great but what you make out of it is left to you alone. All these statements get applied to the Tools being laid out here under for advancing Self as well.

The suggestions made in earlier part were intended to stabilize the mental processes at conscious level with the objective of making mind willing to look deeper, beyond the conscious level. But conscious level working is just the tip of the iceberg as major part of our attitudes and behaviors actually operate at unconscious level. Tools mentioned here are aimed at bringing that very change. The unconscious mind acts as a 'storehouse' of primitive wishes and impulses. The unconscious mind also contains our biologically based instincts for the primitive urges for hunger, sex and aggression, generally labeled as the animal instincts, which are most difficult to be controlled by majority of humanity and for all over its history. But deeper understanding of Self requires access to the core which becomes feasible only when we move over even the unconscious level hurdles, including the burden of our memories, attitudes, behaviors, inhibitions and habits. Practices covered under this section are aimed at opening the door for that very access.

Mastering these critical virtues is life transforming in nature and help making practitioner a better person at every step of his living and in every meaning of the word. These tools are extremely essential for communicating with 'conscience', the inner voice that speaks to us only when we are keen and ready to listen its feeble voice. Conscience speaks to us about justice, moral virtue, humility, honesty and sincerity and every other good thing. It warns against every known negative activity and before we indulge undertaking it. Fortune favors the brave hearts who could refine their receptors and sensors to pick up internal signals and indications resulting in saving themselves from avoiding missteps before damage gets done.

Establishing contact with it, however, is a very subtle art. Its voice also is very lean and frail and can be heard only when noises of everything else in life completely subside making way for the real silence. Being our internal guidance system, once it is properly accessed and functional, it got capacity to answer most of our questions, including questions related to Self. These practices are foundational in nature and there is no escape from mastering them. Let us deliberate each of these practice in little details.

1. Uplifting Moral and Ethical Standards

Understanding Self at this advance stage demands highly elevated moral and ethical standards. Human beings are extremely social species and other people around form a very significant part of their life. Morality and ethics create sustainable environment where mutual interaction among people gets facilitated in an orderly and equitable manner with fairness and mutual respect remaining intact. In its wider context, moral and ethics codes get defined as standards and principles aimed at protecting sense of purity, sanctity, and respect for every living being. An action, thought or words spoken shall be called moral when they do not cause harm or violate individual rights of all others.

The concept of morality is universal in character and all-encompassing in scope. This concept must necessarily operate in all spheres of an individual's life without exceptions. The person can't be selective to be moral while dealing with others and immoral in his personal space. One is either moral or immoral, with no room for a shade of grey in between. Iron cladding of moral and ethics to higher levels is an essential requirement for every person aiming for advancing or shining Self.

Living life normally, these negative traits as well as moral filters remain somewhat dormant. But through repetitive internalization of moral social interactions, morality becomes a well activated faculty and starts regulating person's internal as well as external behavior. Without doubt, people having healthy and functioning moral compass are more grounded, focused, content with life and certainly more productive. They also seem to have more nurturing and positive relationships with external world, people and environment included.

Stricter morality standards practiced over long periods of time develop new neurons in brain helping in cementing moral behavior as a norm. This is no exaggeration as increased frequency of use of any muscle makes it stronger than before. Persistent moral and ethical behavior shines self-awareness, enhances positive self-reflection of our character in self-view boosting self-confidence and self-esteem as well. All this also helps in defending and maturing person's own Self-concept.

Normally, all issues testing our moral behavior operate in momentary episodes and impact only our internal space. That is why people find it easy to downplay their ill effects as rather insignificant. However, these issues hold superlative impact on our psyche. As a default setting, we are wired to feel pricking in inner core with every incidence of moral violation, irrespective of such violation done knowingly or under ignorance. After any immoral or unethical activity, every human being gets bitten by inner conscience. Straight face kept by few does not mean their immoral action has stopped generating pangs of pains, sufferings, regrets and self-tortures. Indulging in immoral or unethical act, therefore, is a sure shot losing preposition. On one side you got a momentary excitation and stimulation but on the other you got to deal with dangerously powerful and long-lasting feelings of guilt and disgust.

Hardships Expected on way to improving Morality

Everybody wishes his morality to shine as pure gold and be appreciated as such by people around. Comparing it with the glittering of gold is a fair expectation so long as one is fully aware how gold arrives to its shining nature. Gold starts its journey without any sparkle, glow or luster and obtains all these attractive qualities on the way following well-defined processes. The ever-captivating glitter identified with gold arrives only at the end of all environmentally challenging processes it goes through to get rid of its associate elements.

In Indian context, the entire concept of Dharma is just an extension of living life with morality. Our critical mental faculty of intellect lets us discriminate and chose. This discrimination and selection of making choice out of options available create conflicts, which are nothing but moral dilemmas for a conscientious person. Attitude applied by a person while making choices goes to determine moral standard of the decision maker. The discussion about Karma Yoga in Bhagwad Gita offers best commentary on the Indian views on morality. Gita differentiates the acts from the intentions and attitudes. Ancient Indian thoughts also equated immorality with sins. Vedas regarded cheating others, arrogance, cruelty, and indolence as sins, while morality laced acts of charity, helping others, hospitality, truthfulness, self-control, chastity, courage, and humility were considered as virtues, which lead a person on the path of Divinity.

Tools for Uplifting Moral Behavior

Having understood the significance of moral and ethical behavior, we must look for proven practices for augmenting such behavior on sustained basis. This is not a new challenge to humanity. This dichotomy had continued all through the recorded history of humanity cutting across cultures and civilizations. Purifying individual's moral and ethical self requires refinement for every word spoken, every idea thought, and every action undertaken. Luckily, pursuing redundancy for these weaknesses is difficult only to begin with. There are some very sweet low hanging fruits in the initial period itself. Within no time of starting sincere efforts, one may expect to get real inner encouragement for spotting and avoiding these weaknesses progressively. Subsequent hardships are not felt as insurmountable.

Person's value system gets expanded and deepened with growth on path of self exploration. The first step to strengthen morality is to make normal behavior congruent with values. Incongruence results in conflicts, confusions, anxiety and even depression. One should review his values with full convictions and clarity which is best done by writing down such values and refining them until clarity emerges. Also, make list of your behavioral patterns under different situations and establish the areas where behavior is not in line with values. Similarly, you must frame out your own individual ethical statement as a written declaration of your closely held principles. This statement must be referred for every step of setting priority, decision making and goal setting exercises.

While working out on your values and ethical statement, please ensure that you address the 'why' part so as to deepen your understanding of your core. You have to have an individual sense of what it means to be moral. And this sense building cannot be emulated. For example, you may find that you have been following some beliefs that are outdated or counterproductive. Show strength to redefine all such beliefs and make amend with conviction. In most other spheres you are asked to be flexible but for morality, you have to take away flexibility and bring in certain amount of uncompromising rigidity. Holding a firm opinion or view about morality may also be unpopular and invite criticism even from people in your close circle but you have to gather courage to pursue even unpleasant course of action.

Expanding your horizon to long term is yet another recommended move to improve morality and ethics. You must operate with a compass that is able to guide you much beyond few miles in front. Expand it to global proportions and get guided for actions that are for the good of all. Look at this world as extension of your own internal system. It is always good to guard against hate, judgments, being unfair, being superficial, resenting towards others or being self-centered. Remain patient in the process and be ready for long haul as morality can't be improved overnight. It is a multi-stage climb and you cannot jump over or over speed to hasten the process.

Yet another recommendation to work on ethics and morality is to strongly defeat the internal enemy of irrationality. Commit yourself to practice being rational at all times. You must become a critical thinker and respond with care and without over-reaction of any type. Be curious like a scientist looking for an unknown good thing that must be found.

2. Propagate Virtue of Compassion

Modern day life generates and inflates many undesirable vices like stress, comparisons, anger, envy and greed. This brings in conflicts with others around. Internet-based connectivity, faceless socializing and pandemics have further contributed a deep void for real social interactions like never before. Notwithstanding everything happening, deep-down human beings continue to remain social animals where happiness has no value unless shared with known circle and celebrations are meaningless without people being around. This loaded imperative on people reaffirm relevance of compassion even today. Compassion refers to extending our actual support to mitigate sorrows and miseries of others; to feel their sorrows as our own. Compassion has the power to connect all human beings by breaking all known boundaries. Compassion is also a state of mind where there is peace for self as well all others around.

On one hand compassion means giving up aggression of every shade while on other hand it means genuinely desiring freedom from pains for everyone around. It originates from the realization that we are all connected with each other and all of us deserve to be free from miseries and sufferings; it brings down all walls between friends and enemies. The real compassion emerges out of the understanding that everyone shares the world and has similar rights to live life. Sense of equality and commonality allows the affinity to permeate in interactions with others around. In a way, well developed compassion injects positivity in our attitude. This positivity starts chain reactions where many of the earlier interpersonal tensions like rivalry, envy, comparisons, and competition are replaced by tolerance, love, acceptance and oneness, in the same order.

As a byproduct, people having compassionate attitude enjoy better psychological and emotional health also as it induces a calmer mind, enhances joy and eliminates stress and depressions. Most importantly, virtue of compassion can be fostered. Taking baby steps, you can start being compassionate with people in your close circle and slowly widen the scope covering even total strangers. But it should be practiced for good will and not for good feelings. Self-seeking in any way make it a tainted effort and, hence, abundant care is suggested for working on compassion beyond the obvious generosity. Size of your activities, however, is less important provided what you do is significant and is commensurate to your worth.

3. Augment Quotient of Empathy

Empathy helps in finding space for establishing trust and faith every time one interacts with others. This approach yields result in the worst of political, social or historical stalemates. This interlinking with others, bridges all differences among human beings be it education, money, power, positions or social status. Modern day life of comforts and luxuries, unfortunately, insulates us from sufferings of others as we become agreeable for own welfare to the exclusion of others.

Improving empathy quotient requires confrontation with your hidden biases with respect to age, gender, status, caste, region, language spoken, religion followed, education, profession and such other man-made divisions. Virtue of empathy helps you suitably respond to all actions, responses, outbursts of others. While other people are source of agony and anxieties in normal state, with improved empathy those very people become support system for enjoying being human in its full potential.

As a matter of relief, studies suggest that tendencies making us less empathetic are not innate but mostly learned. This provide hope that it can be corrected by unlearning old knowledge. In a world that spends so much time picking at flaws and igniting fear and anger in people, empathy can be a balm offering relief against that very fear and anger. To improve your personal empathy quotient, all you need is to reset your inbuilt Wi-Fi that start connecting common neurons already present in all human minds that communicate with each other. To be effective, this connection with others must be established via emotional brain.

Empathy lets you look at things from perspective of others and let you appreciate why they do what they do. Putting others first is just the right beginning for it. Also, follow your instincts about other people and back your actions accordingly because such instincts are nothing but feedback from common neurons received over said

Wi-Fi and are seldom wrong. Lastly and more importantly, abstain from letting your empathy work on selective basis. Being selective on your feelings limits you as a person.

4. Empowering Willpower

In modern days, Willpower is aptly branded as the psychological science of self-control. It is a mysterious pill to ensure right life style, right eating, right thinking and what not. Lack of willpower is also acknowledged as most significant barrier to bring desired changes out of right initiatives. This magic pill is correctly identified with positive life outcomes such as better grades, higher self-esteem, better self-discipline, lower incidence of substance abuse, greater security for resources, and improved physical, mental, and psychological health.

Dr. Kelly Mcgonigal, Ph.D., conducting her class on 'Science of Willpower' at Stanford, opines that willpower is the ability to do what you want to do when part of you really does not want to do it. Willpower is the self-control one exerts to restrain impulses and directing behavior towards chosen goals; the strength helping us decide in favor of what is best for us by resisting the immediate moments of thrill and excitement. For our subject matter of understanding self, the meaning of "Willpower" tilts more towards collective spirit of words like discretion, prudence and discrimination, all rolled into one.

Most befitting and appropriate essence of willpower for our purpose gets captured by the Sanskrit word "Viveka" ("right understanding," "discrimination" or "discriminative knowledge"). It basically differentiates us from animals. Applying Viveka is the ability to differentiate between the real and unreal, eternal and temporary, Self and non-Self, pleasure and bliss alike. Practicing Viveka is a virtue that can be developed and learned by good planning, maintaining good habit and arranging general environment around. Practicing willpower also involves doing a few things and more importantly, not doing many others.

Willpower is like a muscle present in our mind. Some people work on it and make it strong while others ignore it and allow it to go weak. Stronger is this muscle, faster are our strides towards excelling in whatever we do. Strengthening this muscle demands determination and involves setting stretched targets. Interestingly, willpower is a limited resource. It depletes with every use irrespective of the issue being small or big. That is why this critical weapon must be used very selectively, responsibly and judiciously. It is like missiles power of an army which get fired but only after exhausting options of firing bullets, grenades and mortars. This calls for judicious selection of subjects requiring application of your willpower.

Dr. Mcgonigal is also credited to explain willpower as a sum total of three different aspects listed below:

- "I won't" power—the ability to resist temptations.
- "I will" power—the ability to do what needs to be done.
- "I want" power—the awareness of one's long-term goals.

According to her, willpower is harnessing all these three distinct powers to stay out of potential troubles. Failures on the very first aspect are visible in terms of declining moral and ethical standards in general and social curses like addictions, crimes, violence, sexual assaults, etc. in particular. The second aspect contributes to individual's better health, secured relationships, financial value creation, excelling at work/profession and most importantly, remaining happier. Third aspect of focus on long term provides the inspiration to show patience and not settle for small chips at the cost of big coins later. Finally, similar to scoring in school exams, the high-achiever needs to do well in all three areas to be at the top of the class.

Harmless instances like eating that extra portion, pouring that extra peg, skipping exercises on smallest pretext, visiting snacks shops on way to home from Gym, wasting that extra hour on TV, leaving that book in between, oversleeping on Sunday morning, are all common things people do all the time without deeper realizations that all these insignificant looking instances happen to be real enemies of willpower. Each of such instance is nothing but poor self-control. Through these instances you are letting your mind know that 'it is ok to make exception here and there', something that the mind will love to use as often as it likes sending desire for exercising self-control out of the game.

Let us briefly look at a few causes leaking our limited tank of willpower. Wrong eating habits proves to be its first enemy. Food provides energy to the body and mind. Exhausted mind is certainly less receptive for following commands or validating propriety. This is why fatigue is also used as a torture technique. Please eat balanced food, food that releases energy over entire gap between two meals. Please pick up whatever works best for you to ensure you are not running low on energy. Sleep deprivation comes as next enemy of willpower as it dumbs you down. Loss of sleep also pulls down your concentration, it makes your reasoning incoherent, generates mood swings, and disrupts working of your central nervous system. Forget avoiding sleep with the objective of achieving more in less time. Skipping right sleep inevitably messes up more than just your morning mood.

Stress comes as next most common enemy of strong willpower. Stress brings entire attention to immediate at the cost of important. Indulging in vices happens to be yet another enemy of willpower. To remain away from all types of vices and always, is too big a claim for a normal human being. Unfortunately, now innocuous looking addictions like frequent checking of mails, messages, tweets, Instagram posts, Facebook likes/comments and what not are adding insult to injury. All these enemies do appear harmless but who can deny these activities generating avoidable stimulations. Later, that very stimulation manifests itself in the form of strong feelings and emotions operating on extreme levels resulting in desperate thoughts and emotional tensions leading to inner restlessness.

5. Growing Indisputable Acceptance

Finding faults in words spoken by others, expecting others to do things to our liking, own viewpoint being the only right view point, tall expectations from dear ones, taking gestures of others in poor light, pronouncing judgements on others, finding faults with religious/social/political systems/players/groups, are daily life incidences to prove how much non-acceptance exists all around. Living normal social life, it is but impossible to avoid all such situations altogether. But there are three different options for a person to deal with either of such situation. One can either take things 'head on', 'let it go' or 'let it be'. Taking 'head on' leads to confrontations while 'let it go' prove only a temporary solution which is more like postponing the problem or pushing it under the carpet. Beyond any doubt, best choice one should make is to 'let it be'. Arising out of full acceptance, this is the option which does not ignite shades of irritation or frustration.

There is a very nice prayer that describe this situation rather perfectly and it goes as:

> *'God, grant me the serenity to accept the things I cannot change, the courage to change the things I can, and wisdom to know the difference.'* — 'Serenity Prayer',

Acceptance does not mean arguing with reality. Acceptance is choosing to allow it to be there when you cannot change it. Acceptance is about you not struggling against or resisting to or rejecting something causing you undue suffering. Most importantly, it is about making your internal critic get quieter, and in particular, stopping mental agitation caused by actions or words of other people. Acceptance means embracing reality and a willingness to experience things as they are, instead of insisting that they be as you want them to be. How does it help in understanding self? On a more profound level, true acceptance leads to harmony with self which, in turn, makes way for harmony with the whole world. Let it be realized that Acceptance is the only ladder that helps you grow from your 'ego self' to 'true self'.

In reality, non-acceptance does not operate only for external issues as it has far greater consequences for our own individual self. Most of us are not very generous with ourselves and our perceptions about own mistakes, failures, rejections and criticism continue to be our bigger enemies. Non-acceptance of internal issues commands power to elevate our normal worries into nightmares. Non-acceptance enlarges smaller failures into bigger self-doubts and fears. That leads to constant self-judging and ultimately pulls down our self-esteem. Lower self-esteem coupled with internal doubts and fears soon convert into poor emotional and psychological well-being. Self-acceptance, on the other hand is like the process of self-certification that everything is within norms, the syndrome of 'All is well'. This certificate helps a great deal in performing at optimum level.

Acceptance takes out force of negative resistance and makes us receptive for exploration with curiosity rather than anticipation. Acceptance develops padded cells in our mind to absorb vibrations from thoughts thereby minimizing bouncing back effect. Acceptance is like peeling off false and limiting beliefs about self, others and life in general. It removes the very need of negative self-talks, self-control, self-regulation and thereby brings end to useless worries, fears, and anxieties. Non-acceptance, on the other hand, is just like rubber ball, you throw it to the wall with force and it comes back at you with equal force.

As per practical tips from leading psychologists, developing unconditional acceptance for self is the most important part of understanding self. We should begin with a compassionate view toward ourselves and accept all good, bad and even ugly parts as they exist. You can enter into dialogues with your own self imagining you as your best friend. Another way is to write down a letter to your self forgiving past mistakes or live issues bothering you in present. Adopting a growth mindset when facing errors and mistakes is another powerful way to begin.

6. Living in the Present Moment

Reminiscing about past is very common among all people and appears quite natural. Thinking about the past is not so bad as there are many fond memories of the time gone by. The best thing about past is that you very well know about it and there is no uncertainty about it. But the moment past begins to stretch to living in the past, there is a big problem. Even when past is familiar and does not involve surprises, living in the past is absolutely not advisable because it is regressive in nature. Your current version must be better than old version, and if it is not so, there is a bigger problem on hand. Past is largely anti progress, filled with negative experiences and struggles, with just a few recollections of good incidences here and there. Remaining in past is all about recycling and most of what it offers are guilt, remorse, self-doubts or regrets. In any case, past is long gone and is not coming back again. Why should it dictate your present or color your future? Similarly, remaining too busy about future may appear natural and may help make some prudent decisions, but it necessarily involves unfounded imaginations and fantasies generating distressing anxieties and fears.

Present, on the other hand, falls in between past and future. Recommendations for living in present is almost a rage these days and unarguably so because it is backed by sound justifications and actual studies. Remaining in present is awakening to events unfolding in front. Here alone one can live with direct perceptions. Present is fresh, it is real, and it is mesmerizing as it has never happened before. Past is stale and future is figment of imagination. Present can be enjoyed on multi-dimensional scale. In present, everything happens in real time and space. Body, mind, senses, feelings, emotions, thinking are possible to converge together at any subject only when you are grounded in present.

Making use of past to learn can never be questioned but problem arises when people start indulging in glorifying past by reminiscing events to get pleasure all over again. They begin to use glories of the days gone by as yardsticks for measuring present. Even when it sounds like a tiny trivial issue, in the least, it kills the joy of living in present. Likewise, it is good to think about future to avoid mistakes, failures or setbacks about things to come but what to do about associated worries for things unlikely to happen? Let you not forget that every moment spent on past, or future, is at the cost of present and is a losing bargain.

Surely, most people do not observe present as much as they think they do. Right observation of present requires a unique combination of agile sense organs, mental attention and most importantly curiosity of watching something interesting and exciting unfolding in front. It demands conscious awareness for everything happening around. Living in present charges emotional response with positivity pushing stresses away. Focus on present unburdens us from past mistakes or missed opportunities. It also keeps us completely unaware of fallible failures of future. Focus on present also makes us more creative because creativity gets ignited only in present. Being "in the moment" is one of the most significant requirements of understanding your Self.

> *"Touch your inner space, which is nothingness, as silent and empty as the sky; it is your inner sky. Once you settle down in your inner sky, you have come home, and a great maturity arises in your actions, in your behavior. Then whatever you do has grace in it. Then whatever you do is a poetry in itself. You live poetry; your walking becomes dancing, your silence becomes music."* — Osho

Mindful meditation associated with master Thick Nhat Hanh of Vietnamese Zen is strongly recommended for practicing 'being in present'. This practice involves focusing on present moment, accepting and non-judgmentally paying attention to sensations, thoughts and emotions that arise and subside from moment to moment. It can be practiced while doing the most mundane activity of day to day living. For example, you may practice it while, walking, taking bath, watching TV etc. All you do is to watch every moment so closely that there is no spare moment even to comment about it. This technique is also called by other names like 'Present Moment Awareness meditation' or 'Silent Present Moment Awareness'. Interested readers/practitioners are advised to pursue it further depending upon their interest levels. Ajahn Brahm, a very popular British-Australian Theravada Buddhist monk is another famous proponent of Mindful meditation and his books are a good source of this practice.

7. Controlling Mental Distractions

It is normal to experience conflicting thoughts. On one side we feel hungry but another thought suggests to finish the work in hand first. Soon we get reminded to return that important call promised earlier, while yet another thought convinces to check current status of the sporting event running live. These conflicting demands arising at the same time suggest that there are multiple parts within our mind, each simultaneously pushing for its own agenda. Voices responsible for creating such mental interferences, confusions, or diversions, are to be understood as 'distractions' under discussion here.

Distractions must be dealt with squarely before you achieve a conducive state of mind for effective self-exploration of advance proportions. Willingness of the mind is a prerequisite for making headway in such exploration. Innumerable attempts made for comprehending self, without taking care of fragmented or divided mind, are destined for repeated failures and disappointments. Having a distracted mind result in performance of whatever project you working on, and exploration self is no exception. When you do find yourself distracted, it is advised to be aware of why are you getting distracted. Replies obtained for following questions may go a long way to avoid negative impacts of potential distractions and undesired interruptions. Needless to mention, one must be ready to chalk out an actionable plan to ensure that distractions make way for full concentration of both mind and body.

1. How can I spot reasons behind my mind performing in a given situation?
2. Doing a job under compulsion, am I getting distracted because my lack of interest in the job due to it being not in line with my values or goals?

3. Am I trying to perform over my limits? Am I tired physically or mentally? Shall I return back to the work in hand after some gap?
4. Will a change of physical environment, change of scenery, help to achieve desired concentration?
5. Have I lost interest in doing this job because I have been repeating it for too long?
6. Do I lack the skills to do this job as well as some other people do?
7. Am I missing something significant that I wish I was doing instead?
8. Is there any person in particular which is the source of my distractions?
9. Am I getting bored or getting anxiety over quality of the work I am doing?
10. Is my mind waiting for some external feedback or response from someone?

8. Reboot Your Imaginations

Crossing over attachments, pleasures, aversions and fears is mandatory at the advance stage of connecting with Self. And to do that, mind needs to regain its essential and original purity, freshness and receptivity. To begin with, our untrained mind remains influenced of preaching, religious dictates, racial restrictions, and gender generalities and such other obvious categorizations. Long time impact of such divisions necessarily reflects in our habits and attitudes. But at advance stage of explorations, one cannot navigate through without getting rid of all so-called habits and routines simply because the real you may actually be different than your forged version.

People so possessed get stuck in the status quo with no desire to come out of their iron shackles. Getting accustomed to a particular way of living, strong brand consciousness, dependence on specific person, product, routine and habit are all examples of undesired behaviour. How can one take pride in declaring that he is prisoner of such and such thing? Let it be settled then that all systems and habits, even those involving innocent looking insignificant activities, are undesirable and must be pushed out of your system before concluding what is your genuine reality. And you can't make transformational changes without going to your real original version.

Scholars of behavioral psychology identify such roadblocks arising out of 'negative memory' (the interference of previous knowledge with new learning). Old systematic knowledge blocks the way for new learning. In normal life, forgetting old memories and knowledge is considered a curse, a sign of fading memory but for advancing Self, ability to systematically forget old knowledge (including memories), is simply considered a blessing. This sinking of old knowledge is like rebooting one's operating system to go back to original/default settings escaping negative impacts of all types of subsequent system corruptions/virus infections that creep in while operating the software over longer durations.

Going back to default setting allows our mind to regain its innocence making it receptive for fresh knowledge. Else, we get reduced to be robots which are good but only for performing repetitive jobs. Robots can work faster but you do not expect them to use imaginations or activated consciousness. Let us remember that inventions/

innovations become feasible only when logic and imaginations are put into use from new angles. And for that to happen, it is essential to have a routine free, system free, method free, tradition free and belief free mind.

Let us never loose being inquisitive else we are letting go unique potency of logic, reasoning and discretion of being human. History is full of examples where popular and widely followed traditions got extinct from the face of earth because they put imaginations to sleep. Experiments become possible only after moving away from systems of all kinds. The same freedom and flexibility of reasoning, imagining, and discretion is required while attempting to look inward and connect with our real Self.

9. Transcending Ego Beyond Subjectivities

At times, we get brief sense of egolessness in between switching thoughts. It happens for a split second and normal untrained mind generally fails to notice this experience. Lengthening the duration of that very Egolessness happens only after ego loses its hold on its basic spirit of separateness. To put it simply, egolessness is the state where the person feels and act in a manner that self is rendered irrelevant. Meditation practices are known to break through outer layers of ego-defense mechanism.

Once ego is silenced, its menaces of judgement, comparison, and criticism also disappear. This pushes out all negativity and pettiness out of the practitioner's system. Side by side the continued practices of ironclad morality, sustained ethical behavior, stronger compassion, enhanced acceptance, cast-in-steel willpower and other general practices already mentioned, help transcending ego to a level not feasible before.

9

Grasping Mind to Understand Self

Barring few areas, contributions of mind towards success in life outscores contributions of body by miles. Mental strength amplifies all our achievements, success and happiness. Endeavors on 'Understanding and Shining the Self' are equally dependent on that very mental supremacy. As already seen, our attitude, habits, behavior and mental patterns, form the central theme of knowing Self and these all originate and sustained through mind alone.

Let us begin by talking about mind, which incidentally is much more than brain, the physical organ securely sitting in our head. Mind for our purpose is the phenomenon associated with the faculties of sensations, emotions, imaginations, willpower, intuitive memory, and thoughts. In short, everything relating to knowledge and wisdom on one side and abstract issues of feelings and sensations on the other hand, are all associated with mind alone. No wonder, mind continues to baffle people including philosophers, physiologists and psychologists.

Unfortunately, this super critical faculty behaves as a carefree entity always pursuing its own agenda. It rarely likes regulation of any nature. And that is truly the root cause of most of its problems. Solving this very enigma of humanity continues to drive people from all shades to uncover its mysteries and bringing clarity to its working. That is why we are flooded with both scientific and not so scientific researches and theories but without any final word having been spoken about as yet.

Having established the importance of inward mental focus as a critical factor in gaining access to inner core, mastery over working of the mind becomes more critical for its direct connection with consciousness. Length of time and intensity of efforts required to achieve a clear, relaxed, still, alert and willing mind, in the final analysis, determines the roadmap for our entire journey towards our desired destination. Continuing this path necessitates taming this very mind by winning against all its sinister designs.

In this long journey, the first subject to be dealt with involve thoughts in all their manifestations. Thoughts shape our ideas, actions, speech, emotions and precede all our responses, initiatives, actions and reactions. Therefore, all efforts towards nipping the bud must begin with thoughts in terms of their origin, management, regulation or purification. Buddha revealed this very understanding long ago and said, "What we are today is the result of our thoughts of yesterday." Our thoughts of today indeed shape our tomorrow, and thereby our entire future.

Understanding the Mind

Ancient Indian texts deal with human mind related complexities in great details. Mind is said to have 'free will' that is independent of all causes, both consciously as well as unconsciously; it can work based on stored experiences or impressions from past and present or independently of all that. Mind is also not limited in terms of time, space or any other known dimension. These texts further segregate mind into several levels/subparts/forms, namely, Ahamkara, Chitta, Manas, Buddhi and finally Jnana. Much beyond, the physical matter component, all these subtle levels of mind prove the concept of 'mind' under discussion being entirely different from brain, which is purely and undoubtedly a physical organ of human body.

Ancient Indian texts also suggest mind operating under distinct states of Sushupti (unconscious), Nidra (sleep with dreams), Jagruti (Wakefulness), Tureeyam (Trance), Tureeya Ateeta (Para-trance) and finally Ananda (Super consciousness). Consciousness, which is completely independent of both brain and body, is just an aspect of 'mind'. Faculty of consciousness holds complete influence over imaginations, recognitions, judgements, and memories experienced all through mortal life. More importantly, it is responsible for processing all our feelings and emotions before actions get initiated in our mind and body combine. Above mental faculties and states need their own detailed comprehension far beyond the scope of this book. Idea here is just to ignite required inquisitiveness among readers. Let us just begin by saying that every reference to 'mind' in this section shall mean this very complex entity called consciousness with all its levels and states duly included.

How does mind work and why should we spend so much attention on its working? Well, 'it feels good while doing things it likes, when and how it likes'. But the moment you wish to interfere or regulate or suggest it to work in a particular manner, off it goes. Also, mind hates being asked to remain focused on a single subject/object for longer moments as its basic DNA lies in constantly flying from one thought to another. And, unlike common presumption, since most minds are similar, making generalized assumptions about human mind is not out of place. Also, average human mind generally adores simplicity and likes to avoid complexities of all sorts and at most occasions. Its unevolved version is generally lazy, ignores long term implications, and yearns for quick conclusions to avoid hard work.

Going beyond obvious optics, working of human mind involves many layers of processes and systems or we can say that a mind has several other subparts which deal with distinct processes but operating in a complex interconnected manner. Some parts of the mind are responsible for processing sensory stimuli, others deal with memories, predictions, analytical, emotional, while yet another remain engaged in recording like a personal secretary in an office set up. At any given point of time, some of these parts control types of information flow, while other parts integrate and act upon information processed elsewhere to generate executive decisions. Constant flow of new sensations reaching it through smells, sounds, visuals, tastes besides its own interplay of feelings and emotions, keep a mind always occupied.

All these subparts/processes have their own agenda which is seldom in harmony with agendas of other processes. Only on rare occasions, these processes operate with consensus. Seeking mind's attention, on priority ahead of all others, happens to be the top driving force among all these competing processes. Their agenda get pushed constantly even when mind refuse to take notice of earlier stimuli pushed by that process. Different stimuli getting projected on a single subject by competing processes give rise to familiar scenarios of daily life called dilemmas, conflicts and contradictions. Establishing harmony and collaboration within this chaotic, complex and multipart systems, consistently and cohesively, requires crossing over a long, high and scary bridge. And real efforts aimed at training or regulating of this mind exist but only on the other side of said bridge. Certainly, crossing that bridge requires an entirely fresh approach.

Incidentally, Self, our subject of focus, is not a subtle essence existing within this clustered mind because that will make it subservient to mind. On the other hand, Self also does not reside outside mind. It enjoys very special relationship with the mind where, once it is properly realized, Self begins to influence entire thought process. An empowered and realized Self is capable of regulating thoughts in mind but Self itself cannot be thought through by the mind. It is different matter that among normal people with undeveloped Self, the same mind continues to have capability of reducing the powers of Self to self, the ego principle. As we may already realize, this tectonic shift appears small but involves so many transformations that not everyone is able to cover this distance in one lifetime.

Understanding Segregations of Mind: Conscious, Subconscious and Unconscious

Like every other complex entity, for its deeper comprehension, we also get prompted to look at several of its segregations, for example, conscious vs subconscious, left vs right, new vs old, controlled vs automatic, emotional vs rational, and many more. Each of these segregations have their own theories and proponents. But for our specific purpose in hand, its segregation under Conscious, Sub-conscious and Unconscious, merits deeper comprehension. A conceptual look of these three segments will look like a triangle where the peak belongs to Conscious mind, middle portion to Sub-conscious and bottom base to Unconscious. Let us look at each of these sub-parts one at a time.

Conscious Mind

It receives and processes all sensory inputs, identifies patterns, makes decisions and controls short term memory. As a captain in command, Conscious Mind is responsible for communication with outside world as well as other systems within the body. But it has limited capacity, short-term memory and can entertain only one thought at a time. Freud used the famous metaphor of an iceberg to describe the aspects of minds and compared the tip of the iceberg that extends above the water with the conscious mind. Conscious mind also hosts all thoughts, ideas, perspectives, opinions and beliefs for self as well as the world around.

In normal scenarios, undesirable thoughts occupy attention of conscious mind of the ignorant being. In addition, those thoughts keep playing in endless loop like a broken cassette player. Common sight of poor imagination, dull responses, tired memory, inability to arrive at fair and timely conclusions, lack of clarity in thinking, are all strong outcome of this very syndrome. Lots of right efforts are required to make Conscious mind strong and capable to pick only desired thoughts, assign them higher priority, and entertain them for longer duration.

Good level of progress on practices mentioned in earlier chapters cumulatively help in strengthening working of conscious mind. With right progress, Conscious mind begins to set its own agenda. Once conscious mind regains its proper authority, other sub-parts are relegated to act as directed. Over longer periods, this simple process bring out wonders of transformational dimensions.

Subconscious Mind

Generally operating in autonomous mode, sub-conscious mind stores and recalls all past information from cumulative stored past impressions and experiences. Working as a powerful layer underneath the conscious mind, it always remains at work on 24/7 basis. When asked by conscious mind, it carry out the instructions without applying any objectivity, reasoning, analysis or criticism; it just obeys the orders, no questions asked. It is that loyal and old time "Ramu Kaka" (domestic servant) who works day and night to make person's behavior fit in a pattern that is consistent with his stored experiences, hopes and desires. It is indeed that fertile soil which germinates a seed put into it without looking at whether the seed is of a flower, tree, creeper, wild bush or a useless weed.

Subconscious mind is also responsible for imaginations and creativity of all types. Interpreted out of old stored patterns, all the intuition or psychic powers arise from subconscious mind itself. Managing everything relating to our habits, is another critical role it plays. Occupying roughly half of total space of our mind, it is like real working platform where everything is executed as directed by conscious mind. Biggest problem with Subconscious mind is that it loves to maintain *status quo* and believes in always playing safe; every time you wish it to do something new, it gets into motion to make you emotionally and physically uncomfortable. Same thing gets repeated when you command it to walk away from set behaviors or kicking out old habits.

To overcome the long shadows of subconscious mind, you have to give yourself permissions to try out new things by deliberately pushing out your doubts or fear of failures and by doing everything possible to enhance your positivity and motivation levels. Other tools helping here include all types of affirmations and visualizations. Moment to moment awareness, Pranayam, and Yoga also cause delay in gratification impact of senses and weakens impact of emotions on responses suggested by subconscious. Other practices also help in augmenting faculties such that the dependence of conscious mind on unconscious reduces drastically. Once that link is made weaker, bringing desired changes suddenly become practical and effective to implement.

Unconscious Mind

Unconscious mind is primarily responsible for operating all our vital body functions for breathing, digestion, sleeping, blood circulation, nervous system, etc. For all these functions, the unconscious part of mind operates independently without much intervention, direction or supervision by the conscious or subconscious minds. Storing millions and millions of our lifelong experiences, perceptions, feelings, and sensations is another important part of its responsibility. Many of these are not easy to recall as the person might have forgotten all about those. It also houses all those repressed and forgotten personal material of past. It is like this store house situated at the dark and deep end somewhere in basement section of our mind.

Equally important contents of this store house are collectively inherited experiences of entire humanity, our genes, for example, automated responses of 'fight or flight' syndromes. Ignition of survival instincts flood you with stimuli at a fast speed and actions get initiated even before conscious mind becomes aware of the same. Unconscious mind also guides and advises the conscious and subconscious parts through its overarching influence on human behavior. As a strong corollary of this working, efforts for bringing changes at Conscious level or Subconscious level are dependent on bringing changes at the Unconscious level. This is the reason that making significant improvements in our decision-making, self-regulation, emotional management and holding attention over longer spans prove so much more difficult.

Patterns of behavior of unconscious mind form so ever slowly. Repeated over and over again, they become as stiff as forged steel. Many of these patterns move from generations to generations and that is why, bringing smallest change at this level requires deep unlearning. No wonder, making changes in behaviours involve tons of perseverance and endurance.

The unconscious is said to serve for two distinct purposes relating to survival and thriving. As a friend, it does everything for our best interest but part of it is programmed with corrupted information. That part often ignites behaviors that we may not desire. Interestingly, ninety percent of the time unconscious mind remains in control of our thoughts and emotions. That is why it hold overarching impact on our entire personality. Becoming consciously aware of the unconscious, therefore, becomes critical. While ultimate decision-making rests with the conscious mind, but if we are not aware of the unconscious, we submit ourselves to self-destructive tendencies and continue making repeated mistakes. Bringing changes in the working of unconscious mind requires you to understand all about mental distractions and ways and means to get over them.

Behavior and personality that we derive from the constant and unique interaction of conflicting psychological forces operating at these three different subparts of our mind makes us a unique persona with singularity. Each of these parts plays an important role in influencing behavior and hence any reverse engineering required for bringing changes will also be possible within their set interactions.

Understanding Emotional and Rational Mind

People attempting regulation of mind often complain that many of their reactions are reflex actions which they find difficult to control. Common examples of this are outbursts ignited by spontaneous situations. Understanding another segregation of human mind under 'emotional' and 'rational' divisions will be of interest for many readers to understand and appreciate such incidences. Emotional mind is said to be more intuitive, thoughtful and subjective while Rational Mind is categorized as logical, analytical and objective. The emotional mind jumps into reaction to any signal far more quickly while the rational mind likes to take a moment or two to check what should be done. Long time back, when survival was more urgent, emotional mind helped human survive many scary circumstances.

Interestingly, there are two very important studies that have contributed a lot towards insights in the working of Emotional and Rational segregations of human mind. Their results are very convincing and provide useful tips in looking at how these findings help us make progress for our purpose. The studies called as 'Cognitive-Experiential Self-Theory', credited to Paul Ekman, and Seymour Epstein focus on how people use two separate systems dominated by 'analytical and rationality' on one side and 'intuition and experimental' on the other extreme. Emotional mind is faster in responding to emerging circumstances both inside and outside. People using this part of brain, come up with quick reactions. But those reactions also suffer from strong sense of uncertainty. Emotional mind reacts to overall situation in a simple but fast manner and does not waste time to wait for complete and detailed view of the situation. Its speed is so fast that the subject does not even enter the conscious space discussed earlier. What matters here is speed and not accuracy or reasoning. The emotional mind takes snapshot of emerging situation and shoots out the first option at its disposal.

On the other hand, the rational mind takes a few moments to grasp and analyze the emerging situation before coming up with a measured response. Articulated thoughts activate the response in a rational dominance scenario in place of feelings and emotions. Rationality allows opportunity for evaluating a new argument or new evidence. That is why people having stronger rational mind do evaluate new ideas freely and remain open to change their belief without much problem.

Exercising Control over Mind

Training the mind is a daring challenge as mind got a bag full of its own contrivances and it works like a defiant friend that does not like to be controlled. It brings distractions, can make you angry leading to frustrations, it can amplify a tiny sensation into a blown-out emotion, and what not. Ask any person sitting in meditation to know how own mind sabotage the entire process. But there is a silver line. Once it knows that the owner is persistent and his desire remains in conscious space over and over again, the same mind comes around and caves in. Once it is tamed down, you can well expect it to convert into an obedient servant. But to see that day, mind needs to be handled with velvet gloves. Strong arm tactics just do not work.

Tuning the mind for learning new knowledge in a willing manner is the very first step of this long process. Ability to develop keen and pure observation without the reflexes of memories and without the attachment with any particular outcome is the key for tuning mind to make agreeable to learn. Exercising control over mind is possible only with the help of an entirely new muscle, called "Focus". Growing this muscle may be as difficult as doubling biceps or reducing midriff to ideal BMI, but there is no other option. Once it grows well, mind achieves its stillness and opens the access to its subtle state. This alone opens the door to heart and illuminates the path for practitioner to walk in steadily deeper and deeper.

The Ideal Situation

The final measure of degree of regulation of mind is a state when both unconscious and subconscious parts are completely receptive to the desires of the conscious part. In this state, there are no misconceptions, illusions or fallacies in any part of the mind. Such mind is free from attachments, emotions, feelings, or attitudes. Such a mind is in equilibrium without any desire for concoctions, exaggerations or falsifications. All obstacles on the way disappear and ego gets transcended into a higher being. New inputs arriving at conscious space, at this stage, are based on pure observation; mental processing is based on logical reasoning grounded on truth alone. This is here that purest form of Self gets realized.

This state is called 'unified state of mind', a state where all its parts/divisions behave like trained horses pulling the chariot with rhythm and speed in desired direction. Unified mind is called regulated mind or trained mind.

10

Understanding Self being Real Self-Realization

> I am other than name, form and action. My nature is ever free! I am Self, the supreme unconditioned Brahman. I am pure Awareness, always non-dual.
>
> —*Adi Shankara, Upadesasahasri 11.7*

Indian spiritual thought provides for Moksha, Self-Realization as the ultimate objective of an awakened human being. While traditional view about Moksha is intellectually stimulating as well as provoking, it fails to fire imaginations of modern-day seekers as such thoughts involves more questions than answers. Developing complete understanding for Self, on the other hand, is true and practical Self-Realization as the individual begins to know who he truly is. That real knowledge of the true Self is nothing but liberating self-realization.

For such a self-realized modern person, understanding Self is the real manifestation of an understanding that people of wisdom also consider as a fulfillment of all the possibilities of an individual's personality and character. Once a person reaches his own understanding, he becomes free from all desires and worldly attachments. He also achieves complete liberation from external pressures, including those coming from family, culture, society, religion or politics. Such a person rises beyond all types of doubts and delusions. This understanding of true Self alone gets established as eternal and unchanging. This very understanding is the journey starting with identification with the ego and ending with identification with the true Self.

Practicing of tools and techniques mentioned under different chapters allows access to your hidden internal spaces, helps in analyzing their contents, and finally enable you to reprogram them in light of newly found truth and reality. That is how real process of mastering Self, gets underway. The realization brings unity between you and your inner self sets in deep understanding that you and your bigger power are one and the same, always connected. This genuine realization leads to substantial benefits in all areas including true career path, improved health, heightened productivity, better focus, silencing of negative thoughts, and improved intuition. Now you get answers to many questions even without making serious efforts. You realize that long chain of perpetually re-framing, re-organizing, re-thinking, re-interpreting, re-considering all opinions, thoughts, feelings and beliefs helped you in evolving as a better individual, that you got purer lens to see internal reality without any qualitative bias.

Now you can abstain from all senses of right or wrong, complete or inadequate, likable of less likable, socially acceptable or not acceptable. This itself bring mountain of change across all relationships at work or at home, with one's family or world at large. Advancing Self enables you to connect with real Yoga in its original sense of 'union' with something bigger. In general, advanced understanding of Self facilitates real grasp about entire life in its uniqueness and help realize its full potential.

At this crucial stage you find landscape of your entire self getting surrounded by lovely flowers, useful trees and multipurpose plants in place of dense shrubs and weeds that were earlier proudly planted, manured, watered and arranged by you with great care and conviction. You realize how you have been flaunting those weeds and bushes to all your friends and social contacts calling them wonderful collection of things grown by you. This stage of self-realization also allows the sinking of feeling as to how uselessly you have been chasing prevailing fashion statements compromising health and happiness in making money that was far above your necessities and spending that money to acquire things you didn't needed. Finally, you are able to see through inevitable titanic disappointments involved in harboring those trends for chasing cheap thrills devoid of any substance.

This itself is culmination of all Karmic balances; rebirth without physical death, a new beginning grounded in reality and connected cosmic consciousness. This itself is nothing but Sat-Chit-Ananda. This is eternal, uncaused and unexcelled Ananda, the infinite bliss. It is here that there is nothing more to learn, nothing more to do and nothing more to gain. This is a stage where desires are fully gratified, all the worlds are obtained and finally there is no difference in mortality or immortality.

Bibliography

Ajahn, Brahm, *Mindfulness, Bliss and Beyond: A Meditator's Handbook*, Wisdom Publications, Boston, 2005.

Armstrong, Karen, *The Great Transformation, The Beginning of Our Religious Traditions*, Anchor Books, 2007

Badrinath, Chaturvedi, *Swami Vivekananda, The Living Vedanta*, Penguin books, 2006.

Bruce Hood, The Self Illusion - How the Social Brain Creates Identity, Oxford University Press, New York, USA, 2012

Bucke, Richard Maurice, *Cosmic Consciousness* : A Study in the Evolution of Human Mind, Dover Publications USA, 2012

Chinmayananda, Swami, *A Manual of Self Unfoldment*, Central Chinmaya Mission Trust, 1975.

Chinmayamamda Swami, Commentary on Atmabodha by Adi Shankaracharya, Central Chinmaya Mission Trust, 2012

Cooper, David A., *A Heart of Stillness—A Complete Guide to Learning the Art of Meditation*, Bell Tower, an imprint of Harmony books, a div. of Random House, Inc, 1999.

Cooper, David A., *Silence Simplicity and Solitude – A complete Guide to Spiritual Retreat*, Bell Tower, an imprint of Harmony books, a div. of Random House, Inc, 1999.

Culadasa (John Yates, Ph.D) and Matthew Immergut, with Jeremy Graves, *The Mind Illuminated, A Complete Meditation Guide Integrating Buddhist Wisdom and Brain Science for Greater Mindfulness*, Touchstone, 2015.

Dalai Lama, His Holiness and Howard C. Cutler, *The Art of Happiness; A Handbook for Living*, Hodder and Stoughton ltd. London, 2009.

Dalai Lama, His Holiness The, *The Path to Freedom*, Abacus London, 2002.

Doniger Wendy, *The Hindus: An Alternate History*, The Penguin Press, New York, 2009.

Dan P. McAdams, Personal Myths and the Making of Self, The Guilford Press, USA, 1993

Deepak Chopra and Means C Kafatos, You Are The Universe – Discovering Your Cosmic Self & Why it Matters, Harmony Books, New York, USA, 2017

Eknath, Easwaran, *Passage Meditation—Bringing the Deep Wisdom of the Heart into Daily Life*, Nilgiri Press, 3rd edition 2010 by Publishing division of blue Mountain Center for Meditation.

Elizabeth Gilbert, Eat Pray and Love, One Women's Search for Everything, Bloomsbury Publishing, London, New York and Berlin, 2007

Elizabeth Gilbert, Committed: A Sceptic Makes Peace with Marriage, Bloomsbury Publishing, London, New York and Berlin, 2010

Gautier, Namrata and Francois Gautier, *The Art of Healing Pranayama: The Breath of Life*, HarperCollins, 2010.

Giri, Swami Satchidananda, *My Struggle for Self-Realization, An Autobiography*, Shipra Publications, 2015.

Goleman, Daniel, *Emotional Intelligence; Why it can matter more than IQ*, Bantam Books, NY, 1996.

Goleman, Daniel, *Social Intelligence: The New Science of Human Relationships*, Bantam Books, NY, 2006.

Hanh, Thich Nhat, *The Art of Mindful Living* (Audio Edition), Sounds True, 1999.

Hart, William, *Vipassana Meditation—The Art of Living as Taught by S.N. Goenka*, Vipassana Research Institute, Dhamma Giri, Igatpuri, Apollo Printing Press, Nashik, 2017.

Jaymesh Shah, Swa-Sanjivani (in Hindi), Jay Satchitananda Sangh, Ahmedabad, India, 2007

Mike Bayer, Best Self – Be You, Only Better, HarperCollins Publisher, New York, 2019

Jonathan, Haidt, *The Happiness Hypothesis—Finding Modern Truth in Ancient Wisdom*, basic books, A Member of the Perseus books group, 2006.

Kempton, Sally, *Meditation for the Love of It; Enjoying Your Own Deepest Experience*, Sounds True, Colorado, 2011.

Krishnamurti, J., *Inward Revolution*, Shabhala Boston and London, 2006.

Lawrence, Richard, *The Meditation Plan; 21 Keys to your inner potential*, Judy Piatkus, London, 1999.

Osho, The Book of Understanding: Creating Your Own Path to freedom, Harmony Books, New York, 2006

Osho, How to Know Yourself, Penguin Random House Pvt. Ltd., India, 2018

Phillip C. McGraw, Self Matters – Creating Your Life from the Inside Out, Free Press, USA, 2001

Sandy C., *Mind Calm–The Modern Day Meditation Technique that gives you 'Peace with Mind'*, Hay House

Radhakrishnan, S., The Principal Upanishads, HarperCollins Publishers, Twenty Second impression, 2011

Radhakrishnan, S., Indian Philosophy, Oxford University Press, Sixteenth impression, 2017

Radhakrishnan, S., *The Hindu View of Life*, HarperCollins, 2009.

Roberts, Bernadette, *What is Self? : A study of the Spiritual Journey in Terms of Consciousness*, Sentient Publications, 2005.

Rebecca Whitecotton, Pull Your Self Together, Capucia LLC, New York USA, 2021

Schneider, Susan and Max Velmans, *The Blackwell Companion to Consciousness*, 2nd Edition, John Wiley and Sons UK, 2017.

Siegel, Daniel J., Md, *Aware—The Science and Practice of Presence, The Ground Breaking Meditation Practice*, A TarcherPerigee book, New York, 2018.

Sivananda, Swami, *Concentration and Meditation,* The divine life Society, Shivanandanagar, 2014.

Tejomayananda, Swami, *Living Vedanta* (Vedanta Cintnam), Chinmaya Prakashan, Mumbai, 2014.

The Shivananda Yoga Vedantic Centre, *The Sivananda Book of Meditation*, Gaia Books.

Tyagi, Ashok, *All About Hinduism–From Vedas to Devas and Past to Present*, Shipra Publications, Delhi, 2015.

Tyagi, Ashok, *All About Spirituality – Practical Way for Self Realization*, Shipra Publications, 2017.

Tyagi Ashok, All About Meditation – Art and Science of Fulfillment and Euphoria, Shipra Publications, 2021

Waitley, Denis, *Empires of the Mind—Lessons to Lead and Succeed in a Knowledge Based World*, Nicholas Brealey Publishing, London, 2004.

Yogananda, Paramhansa, *Autobiography of a Yogi*, Yogoda Satsanga Society of India, 2010.

Articles, Lectures, Essays and Blogs and Various Websites

Various online essays about Human Behavior at www.spiritualsearchfoundation.com

Various articles published on www.scientificamerican.com

Articles about Yoga, Meditation and Ayurveda on www.antaryami.com

Seven Pranayama; breathing exercised by Swami Ramdev hosted at www. atmabodh.net/2015/06/pranayama
True Meditation Evolution's Tools for Ego Transcendence by brad Reynolds at www.integralworld.net/reynolds
Articles about Sadhana under Kundalini Yoga at www.3ho.org/kundalini- yoga/sadhana-daily-spiritual-practice
Various Articles hosted at www.spiritualworld.org
Various articles by V. Jayaram hosted at www.hinduwebsite.com
An overview of 23 different meditational techniques explained by Giovanni at www.liveanddare.com/types-of-meditation
Various articles hosted at www.yogabasics.com
Articles hosted at www.verywellfit.com
Interesting Articles at www.mindtools.com
Article about self understanding at www.liveboldandbloom.com
Articles about Self on www.greatergood.berkeley.edu
Articles at www.psychcentral.com
Life related Articles at www.theschooloflife.com
Self related articles on www.simplypsychology.org
Articles hosted at www.vedanet.com
Articles published at www.positivepsychology.com
Articles published on www.peterfenner.com